Into the Millennium

*20th Century messages
for 21st Century living*

Into the Millennium

20th Century messages
for 21st Century living

IAN R. K. PAISLEY

AMBASSADOR
Belfast • Greenville

Into the Millennium

Copyright © 1998 Ian R. K. Paisley

ISBN 1 84030 025 6

AMBASSADOR PRODUCTIONS LTD,
Providence House
16 Hillview Avenue,
Belfast, BT5 6JR
Northern Ireland

Emerald House,
1 Chick Springs Road, Suite 206
Greenville,
South Carolina 29609
United States of America

Foreword

THE WORLD IS DRIVEN ONWARDS with ever increasing momentum towards the second millennium, the seventh in the history of this present earth.

In the world of sinful man, the anchors are all gone, and he has become the plaything of every storm of hell and tempest of iniquity.

The impregnable Rock of Ages is the only immovable refuge and hiding place as this planet collapses into its final demise.

"Therefore will not we fear, though the earth be removed, and though the mountains be carried into the midst of the sea; Though the waters thereof roar and be troubled, and though the mountains shake with the swelling thereof, Selah." Psalm 46: 2,3.

Amidst the apostasy of the doomed world, the Gospel, the Good News, is still light in the darkness, hope in the despair, joy in the sorrow, help in the trouble, deliverance in the depravity and redemption in the ruin.

These sermons, preached at the opening of each year of the last decade of the century leading up to the millennium, point God's way forward. They beacon forth the light which shineth more and more unto the perfect day.

They are indeed twentieth century sermons for twenty-first century living.

May the God Who enabled me to prepare them and proclaim them use them as their life is prolonged in print.

Yours to serve in the Gospel.

Rev R. K. Paisley

Eph 6:19 +20

March, 1998

Contents

1 The waiting God
and His waiting people

I WANT TO TAKE for our Motto Text for 1990 the eighteenth verse of this thirtieth chapter of Isaiah.

In doing my Bible reading I was greatly struck with this text. We are all familiar with the necessity of God's people to be a waiting people. That is an old truth. It is an old truth which is hard to learn. Would to God we would learn it! Would to God we would practise it!

God is looking for a waiting people.

The thought in this verse however is complementary to the waiting people. This text speaks of the waiting God. Notice it carefully, '*And therefore will the LORD wait, that He may be gracious unto you, and therefore will He be exalted, that He may have mercy upon you: for the LORD is a God of judgment: blessed (or happy) are all they that wait for Him.*'

The waiting God and the waiting people.

You will notice five views of God in this verse. Five in Scripture is the number of grace, and we notice first of all, **the Rationale of the Waiting God.**

Notice that word '*therefore*' There is a reason. There is a reason why God waits. The rationale of a waiting God.

Then notice the second view, '*That HE may be gracious unto you.*' There you have the **Royalty of a Waiting God**. He is going to freely bestow His gifts in a right royal manner upon those that He sees are waiting for Him. The royalty of a waiting God.

Then look at the third view which is the centre view and you have **the Reign of the Waiting God**, '*that He may be exalted.*' He is reigning, He is uplifted, He is on the Throne. Of course, we have here the emphasis on His exaltation, when He was lifted up on a Cross. God bestows everything upon us because Christ was lifted up, '*And if I be lifted up I will draw all men unto me.*'

Then look at the fourth view, '*That He may have mercy upon you.*' There you have **the Redemption of the Waiting God.**

The final view is **the Righteousness of the Waiting God**, '*For the LORD is a God of judgment*' - Righteousness! Five views of the God Who is waiting.

THE FIVE-FOLD ARGUMENT

I want you to notice something, that all those views of God are an argument for you to wait upon God. If He is working out His plan, His reason and that is why He is waiting, then we can say, 'Blessed are all they that wait for Him,' and they wait for Him *expectantly*. If God has a purpose and a plan in waiting, then I can be blessed as I wait upon Him expectantly.

But if God exercises and displays His royalty as a waiting God, then it can be said, 'Blessed are all those that wait upon Him *exceptionally.*'

We should exceptionally wait upon God. Our prayers should be exceptional prayers. So often our prayers are mundane, common-place, the stringing of repeated sentences, the smell of the mothball is on them.

In the old days they put mothballs in the wardrobes. You only wore your good suit on Sunday and when you put it away on Sunday night you put the mothballs in. When you brought it out the next Sunday it smelt of mothballs. When you went to Church the whole Church smelt like a mothball.

Of course, you young people would not know anything about mothballs. It is only the old greyheaded people who have false teeth, it is only they that know something about moth balls. There are prayers and they are like moth-balled clothes.

If however, we get the vision this morning of the royalty of the waiting God, we will pray exceptional prayers.

It is a wonderful thing when you hear exceptional praying. I was in a prayer meeting one night with Rev W P Nicholson. There was a man praying an exceptional prayer. He was not doing it intentionally. He was doing it ignorantly. He tried to quote that passage of Scripture in Habakkuk, 'LORD, make my feet like hinds' feet.' He got a bit mixed up and said, 'LORD, make my feet like hens' feet.' Nicholson roared, 'Glory to God, you will never back-slide. I never saw a hen walking backwards yet.'

It was an exceptional prayer! If you pray with your eye on a royal God you will pray exceptionally.

I was reading C T Studd and he was in the heart of Africa and he was reading one night aided by an old oil lamp. He read, 'every place that your foot shall tread upon shall be yours,' and he yelled out, 'God, give me big feet.' That was an exceptional prayer, but God gave him big feet. He had his eye on a royal God. Our prayers will be exceptional.

Thirdly, if you have your eye upon the reign of the Waiting God you will pray not only expectantly and exceptionally, but you will pray *exaltedly*. There will be an exaltation in your prayers. Man, you will not pray as if you were half dead or sleeping and you had not the cobwebs out of your eyes. You will be praying with an exaltation in your heart.

Then if you have your eye upon the Redemption of the Waiting God; that God is going to bless you, you will be praying *exclusively* to God. You will not be looking anywhere else for a blessing, you will be sold out exclusively on God.

I love to hear a Christian saying, 'I am going to pray about that,' because that Christian has learned that it is only prayer to God exclusively which can bring the answer.

Then if you have your eye on the Righteousness of a Waiting God, you will pray *exactly*. There will be a definiteness, an exactness and honesty about your praying, if you have your eye on the righteous God.

I. THE RATIONALE OF THE WAITING GOD

Let us go back and look at the rationale - the reason of a waiting God. *'Therefore.'* The children of Israel in this chapter were in a bad state. They were about to face the worst defeat in all their history. Instead of looking to God they were looking everywhere but to God.

That is like the church today, is it not? Instead of looking to God in prayer we talk about getting new methods, we talk about trying to attract people, trying to fill vacant seats by worldly methods with Saul's armour upon us instead of going back to the basics of praying.

The Lord said, 'I am going to bring you low, I am going to teach you a lesson, you are going to be left as a beacon, (look at verse 17) upon the top of a mountain, and an ensign on a hill.' That word 'beacon on top of a mountain,' is 'a tree bereft of its branches.' You are going to be left like that. What was God doing? He was cutting the feet from under them because of their sinful self-confidence. When people have confidence in themselves then that is the reason that God waits.

God has been delaying intervention in our own Province, I wonder why? We have prayed for deliverance but deliverance has tarried. We have cried for revival, but revival has lingered. We have prayed for our unsaved loved ones, but today they are still in their sin. What is God doing? He is teaching us that there is a time when He works. He wants to take away all our self-confidence. Did you look at that verse 15 in Isaiah 30? *'In returning and rest shall ye be saved: in quietness and in confidence shall be your strength: and ye would not.'*

No, the people of God do not want to return to God in prayer, they do not want to rest only in the Lord, they do not want to be quiet and confident in a Sovereign, Waiting God.

Thank God, blessed are all those that wait on him **expectantly**. I have got an expectancy in my heart. There is a purpose why God delays. There is a purpose why God seems to be slow. There is a purpose why God does not make haste. I can pray expectantly.

'Unanswered yet the prayers your lips have offered,
In agony of heart these many years,

Say not, the Father hath not heard your prayer,
You shall have your desire, some time, somewhere.'
You can pray **expectantly**, for God has a rationale for His waiting.

II. THE ROYALTY OF THE WAITING GOD

Let us turn to the second one, the royalty of the Waiting God, *'That He may be gracious unto you.'*

What is grace? Grace is the free, undeserved, unmerited favour of God. Let me tell you, I have heard preachers preach and they have said, 'You can buy revival if you pay the price.' That is untrue. That is a heresy. There is no such thing as buying revival. There is no such thing as being able to pay God the price of His blessing. Any blessings I ever have I get them because of free grace alone. *'That He may be gracious unto you.'* Here we have the royalty of a Waiting God. He is not going to bless us because we deserve it. He is not going to bless us because we have purchased it. He is not going to bless us because we have reached a certain standard. No, He is going to bless us because He is a God of grace.

Turn to Isaiah chapter 64 verse 4. This is an amazing verse which burned its way into my heart when I was meditating this week in the Cameroon. What a verse it is! Isaiah chapter 64, verse 4, Listen to this, *'For since the beginning of the world men have not heard, nor perceived by the ear, neither hath the eye seen, O God, beside Thee, what He hath prepared for him that waiteth for Him.'* There is the God of grace speaking. He promises that since the beginning of the world, no eye hath seen, no ear hath heard, neither hath it entered into the heart of man, what God will give to the person who waits on Him. It is time you started waiting.

Your spiritual life is low. You are impoverished. You are in rags today, You are not the man or woman of God you ought to be. Start waiting upon the Lord, and God will reverse the whole process of backsliding and declension. Wait upon the Lord! Eye hath not seen, ear hath not heard. Oh, the royalty of a waiting God. Let us start praying exceptional prayers. Do not pray for little things, pray for big things.

I had an old Hebrew Professor, and he wrote me a little note before I was ordained to the Christian ministry on this Road. He said, 'Dear brother,

Expect great things from God, and then go out and attempt great things for God.' It was William Carey who first wrote those words, Expect great things from God, attempt great things for God,' for God is a God of royalty.

III. THE REIGN OF THE WAITING GOD

Look at the third one, The Reign of a Waiting God, "He will be exalted.' That is right in the centre. The third one in any Scripture five, is the centre. It is the all important one. An exalted, reigning God! I am glad God reigns today, are you not? I am glad God is on the Throne today. I am glad a waiting God occupies the Heavens.

There was a great skit on Sunday Sequence this morning on Fundamentalists of all kinds. You would think they were funny mentally as well, to listen to that programme. I am glad, my friend, that I believe in this Book. I do not care whether people laugh at it or not. I do not care how they poke fun at God's Book, for God is on the Throne. He is the God who reigns. I laugh when I listen to these people because they are only grasshoppers. There are certainly a lot of grasshoppers around the BBC, a lot of grasshoppers, but I tell you, everything in this book will be fulfilled.

They bring on the so-called scholars. They line them up. These educated idiots tell you, 'Of course, nobody really believes the Bible today.' Thank God, I believe the Bible! I will tell you what is more, the devil has enough sense to believe the Bible, for the devils believe and tremble. The very devil knows that this Bible will be fulfilled. When Jesus Christ said, 'It is written' the devil shut his mouth. He had nothing more to say.

Let me tell you, God is exalted. He is on the Throne, and if that is true, then I can wait upon God with an exalted spirit. We are on the winning side. we cannot be defeated. We are going to win this battle.

Some people ask us, 'What is going to happen to the world?' I will tell you what is going to happen to the world. The Lord our God is coming back again, and the Christians are going to reign over the world.

It will be nice to put Bush out of the White House, will it not?, and to occupy it. To put the Pope out of the Vatican and occupy it.

I have often said that I am asking God for rulership of two cities, Dublin and Rome in the millennium.

I would just like to rule over them during the Lord's reign upon the earth. Needless to say, I would make a few changes. There would be no nuns after I would be there!

Let me tell you something, we are to pray exaltingly. You have got to have confidence in the God who answers your prayers. If I did not believe that God was on the Throne, if I did not believe a Holy God was going to work out everything after this Book, I would not stand in the pulpit. Thank God, I believe it. Every bit of it will be fulfilled. Hallelujah! Even the bits I do not understand, they will all be fulfilled.

You start praying exaltingly. Get down on your knees. Wipe the shame and the unbelief out of your heart and start praying exaltingly. God can do everything. When the Syrians came to take over Jerusalem, Isaiah prayed a prayer and he said to Hezekiah, 'Do not worry any more,' and two hundred thousand soldiers were corpses overnight. He never had to draw a sword or fire an arrow. God can wipe out His enemies.

You remember the Lord said that the Father could send Him ten legions of angels, that is about ten million of them.

God can do all things. It is about time you got the eye of faith on an exalted God and started praying, is it not? Pray *exceptionally, expectantly, exaltingly.*

IV. THE REDEMPTION OF THE WAITING GOD

Then we have the redemption of the waiting God. *'He will have mercy.'* I love that!

I was thinking today that the highest and most holy part of the typology of the Mosaic economy was the blood-sprinkled mercy seat. That is what it was. Why? God is a God of mercy. He is the waiting God of mercy.

I will tell you something, we are to come boldly to the throne of grace, where we can obtain mercy and find grace to help in the time of need. What a promise!

God's people dilly dally. They will not come to the prayer meetings. They are a prayerless, graceless crowd, the Christians of today. They do not pray. They do not seek God.

How God must look at them and say, 'You draw near to me with your lips, but your heart is far from me.'

The waiting God is a God of Redemption. He is a God of Blood. He is a God of Expiation. He is a God of Cleansing. He is a God who Redeems. I am going to pray to Him *exclusively*. I have no other place to go but to the Throne of grace.

Where will I go when I am in trouble? Run to my neighbours? Run to my friends? Run to the preacher? Do not be a fool. They can do no more for you than anyone else. You run to God.

The sign of a man walking with God is the fact that when he is in trouble he runs to his God.

The first thing I do when I am in trouble, I run to God. I do not sit down and say, 'I will make that move and this move, and the other move and work it all out,' I just go to God and say, 'Lord, you take care of it. It is beyond me, but you are the God of redemption. You are the God of mercy. You are the God who redeems.'

What is redemption? It is a buying back. Thank God He can redeem the time for you. He can redeem your life. He can restore the years that the locusts have eaten.

Some of you are moaning and groaning over past failures. You know what you need to do, friend? Take your eye off the past and get your eye on the Lord. He can reverse the failures. He is the God Who reverses failures.

John Mark was a failure, and he became the writer of that beautiful Gospel which bears his name - the Gospel of Mark. He was the man who fell, but praise God he rose again. Thank God you can rise again.

Jonah was a failure. He ran away, and instead of eating fish the fish ate him. Yes, he was the bit of a cod in the fish's belly. Then God told the fish to vomit him up. You can see him covered with the stomach juices of the fish's belly. Did you ever see such a sight?

The Lord taught him a lesson, He did! He came out and he was terrible, a pathetic sight. He rubbed himself down and said, 'What a sight I am!' but he went and preached.

When he got there he was still as stubborn as ever. He was the only preacher to whom God gave revival to and he did not want it. God saved the whole city and he did not want it. Instead he sat down and sulked. There is something more despicable than a child that sulks, and it is a man or woman who sulks. That is worse than a child sulking.

There are a lot of sulkers in the church today. They do not like what God is doing. God caused a large mushroom to grow, and it put a shade on his head and he sat under it. He said, 'It is nice and cool here.' Then God took the mushroom away, and he did not have mushroom soup either!

Rather, he sat there in misery. God said, 'You liked the mushroom, but you never worked to get it, and I took it away. You had more thought for a mushroom that you had for the men and women and children and beasts of Nineveh.'

God taught Jonah a lesson! But the secret of Jonah's life was, he said, in the fish's belly, 'I will look again.' Thank God, you can always look again to Calvary. Thank God, you can always look again to the Cross. You should pray exclusively!

V. THE RIGHTEOUSNESS OF THE WAITING GOD

Finally, the Righteousness of the Waiting God. He is a God of judgment. We should pray *exactly*, 'Lord, honour your word, dot every 'i,' stroke every 't,' you are a God of judgment.'

God will do the right thing. Do you remember Abraham? Abraham prayed. Did you ever ask yourself why he prayed just down to the number ten, and then left off praying? I will tell you. He had counted all the family of Lot, and concluded, 'There are ten of them, and maybe they are all righteous.' There was in fact only one righteous man, not ten.

Do you know what Abraham said? 'Shall not the Judge of all the earth do right?'

When you come to God you are praying to a God of judgment. 'Blessed are all them that wait upon Him exactly.' What God says in this Book about Rome, He will fulfil every Word of it. What God says about Communism in this Book, He will fulfil every Word of it. What God says about the old Harlot Church and Ecumenism, He will fulfil every Word of it. What God says about His people, He will fulfil every Word of it. He is a God of judgment. God will rise up in this earth. His day is coming. God has a time, and God's time is approaching. 'Blessed are all they that wait for Him.'

Are you going to start waiting for him today? I trust this sermon will revolutionise your praying! I trust when you kneel down to pray, it will not be the old moth ball sentences you will spill out of your mouth, but you will start really praying, laying hold upon God, seeking God, crying upon God. I pray that this church will become a waiting church, and as we wait God will do something that the eye of man hath not seen, the ear of man hath not heard, neither hath the heart of man conceived.

AMEN AND AMEN!

2 Stirring up our *memories*

OUR 1991 MOTTO TEXT is found in the book of Deuteronomy chapter eight verse 2.

At the beginning of each new year it is our custom to take a text and make it our Motto Text for that particular year. For the Free Presbyterian Church this year is an extra special year. We celebrate our 40th anniversary. As you know, in the last Lord's Day of March we will be having all our churches congregating in a great conventicle in the King's Hall at Balmoral. All our services across Ulster and in the South of Ireland will be coming to that great conventicle. We are looking forward to that with all our hearts.

On 17th March, 1951, that was the day the Free Presbyterian Church was born in Crossgar. On that Sabbath we will be bringing our children to our services and we will be presenting every child with a special anniversary Bible. The Bibles will be autographed by myself and Dr. John Douglas as Clerk of Presbytery.

Seeing this was the 40th anniversary I thought I could do no better than to pick for the motto text verse two of the eighth chapter of Deuteronomy, *"And thou shalt remember all the way which the Lord thy God led thee these forty years in the wilderness to humble thee, and to prove thee, to know what was in thine heart, whether thou wouldest keep his commandments or no."*

Old man Moses is here singing his swansong. Moses was a great singer and a unique soloist. He sang the first song that is recorded in the Bible. You will find it in Exodus 15. He also wrote a special song which is incorporated in the Book of Psalms, it is Psalm 90. He is given the greatest honour that can be given to any person, his name is eternally linked with the Lord Jesus and in heaven, according to Revelation 15:3 you will sing the song of Moses and of the Lamb. So Moses was a great singer.

This is part of his swansong. It is filled with intense earnestness, because at the end of 120 years Moses had not a sign of old age about him. His eye was not dimmed and none of his natural force had abated.

He knew the temptations the children of Israel would face. He knew their weaknesses for he had experienced for 40 years their stubborn obstinacy against God, their violation of God's commandments and their determination to go against the commands and will of God. So he applied practical earnestness to his final exhortation to the children of Israel.

It was a motivated earnestness, for he was looking at the past 40 years and every trial that he had come through with the people of God; every battle that had been fought for their safety and encouragement and protection; every miracle that God had wrought for them, intervening time and time again to deliver them. All those motivated old Moses as he sang his swansong.

If you read it you will discover that Moses did not trust to legal bands to hold him and his people to God. He trusted in the love bands of God and he emphasises over and more, over and over again, the mighty love of God.

The only thing that will keep you close to the side of your Lord this year will not be legal bands but it will be the love bands of the Saviour. The bands that are crimsoned with the blood of His Divine Redeeming.

Having said that by way of introduction, I want to underscore six things that they were to remember and these six things are common to us this morning.

ONE: A PERSONAL GOD

You are to remember, Moses said to the children of Israel, that you have a personal God. Every one of us who is redeemed by the Saviour's blood need to remember that today - we have a personal God. Look at the text, *"the Lord thy God"*. Remember you have a personal God. That is relationship, the emphasis is on relationship. You have a personal God.

It is by a personal act of God that you have a personal God. If you read what Moses said, it was not because of their righteousness, it was not because of their numbers, it was not because of anything resident in their hearts that the Lord was their God. It was only because of His great personal choice.

There is an old hymn that says-

What was there in me
That could merit esteem
Or give the Creator delight
T'was even so Father
I ever must sing
Because it seemeth good
In thy sight.

The love of God, the sovereign love of God. This is no ordinary love. We rejoice in the love of wife, we rejoice in the love of mother and father, we rejoice in the love of son and daughter and brother and sister, we rejoice in every expression of love manifested on the human level, but put all of those loves at their highest and deepest and broadest together, and they are not to be compared for one moment to the love of God. We are loved by God with the very same love with which He loves His Only Begotten Son.

So dear, so very dear to God,
Dearer I cannot be
The love with which He loves His Son
That love extends to me.

With one difference. That it seems to me that His love for me is more in one instance than it was to His son. You say, "Preacher, you are treading on dangerous ground." No I am not. I am treading on Scriptural ground for I read in this Bible that He spared me but He did not spare His Son. God spared not His own Son. So when His eye lit upon Christ instead of me He made a choice. He ordained that His Son should go to that cross of ignominy and shame and that I should be freed to walk in the paths of righteousness and to come to the everlasting glory of the eternal city of the Triune Jehovah.

This is love that passeth knowledge and all understanding. If the love of the Father is so wonderful what about the love of the Son. Measure it by the measuring rod of the cross. Count the drops of blood that ooze from His thorn-crowned brow. Count the blood that flows from His lacerated back. Count the flow of blood from His hands and from His feet and see that great fountain that flowed from His precious bleeding side. Listen to His own words, "having loved His own, He loved them unto the end."

Oh the deep, deep, love of Jesus,
Vast, unmeasured, boundless, free,
Rolling like a mighty ocean
In its fullness over me.

What of the love of the Spirit who came down to this earth, stained, soiled and scarred and sought me out among millions of folks upon this planet and entered into my sin-cursed heart and worked a work of grace in regeneration of my soul.

My friend, this is love so amazing and do divine and it is that love that gives us a personal God. Remember you have a personal God.

TWO: A PERSONAL GOD LEADING YOU

Secondly, remember you have a personal God leading you. *"Thou shalt remember all the way which the Lord thy God led thee."* There is the emphasis on leadership. A personal God has its emphasis on relationship. A leading God has its emphasis on leadership.

You would need a well tuned harp to play the praises of a God who leads us. What a wonderful thing that the child of God can whisper in the darkest hour - He leadeth me.

I was saying to those men in the prison today, some of them are lifers, some of them have committed murder, some of them are incarcerated for various and grievous crimes of blood, I was saying to them today that God has preserved you to this very service in order that you might be redeemed and saved by the grace of God. I am amazed how God looks after sinners before they are converted in order that they may be brought savingly to Himself. I never think of that but I think of the old hymn

Indulgent God, how kind
Are all Thy ways to me,
Whose dark finitely mind
Was enmity with Thee.
Yet now subdued by sovereign grace
My spirit longs for Thine embrace
Preserved in Jesus
When my feet made haste to hell
There I would have gone
But Thou hast done all things well.
Thy love was great,
Thy grace was free,
Which from hell's pit
Delivered me.

The Lord led you in your unconverted days to bring you to the place of conversion and salvation. If He led you in your unconverted days He has led you since you knew Him as a personal God and what a way He has led us. What a path He has brought us by, all His ways are pleasantness and all His paths are peace.

THREE: A PERSONAL GOD LEADING YOU THROUGH THE WILDERNESS

Thirdly, remember you have a personal God leading you through the wilderness and the emphasis is on the wilderness and that is hardship. The wilderness was no easy way. Would you ask yourself a personal question today. How did I come to where I am? You have come to where you are, child of God, because a personal God has led you through this old weary wilderness of the world. In your unconverted days if someone had told you you would be sitting in God's house, with God's love in your heart, singing the praises of Divine redemption and rejoicing in prayer and Bible reading, you would have sneered. There are men here now converted to God and they would have blasphemed with a string of blasphemy if you suggested that they would ever become Christians. Today you are a child of God through the grace of God, and through the hardness of the wilderness He has brought you. Sometimes the track has been as narrow as a razor edge. Sometimes you have been led into darkness, you have been led through the depths, you have been led through the furnace and through the loneliness, but God has made miracle after miracle happen to you and today you are here and the wilderness journey is behind you, for God has brought you through the hard way. In the wilderness there were serpents, enemies, and we have all faced the enemy and we have all encountered serpents by the way.

It is not an easy road we are travelling to heaven, it is a wilderness way. But thank God there is One that brightens the journey and lightens the load for us. We have a personal God, that is relationship. We have a personal God leading us, that is leadership. We have a personal God who brings us through the wilderness, that is hardship.

FOUR: A PERSONAL GOD LEADING YOU FORTY YEARS

But notice again Moses said, you have a personal God leading you for forty years, notice the emphasis on the forty years. That is companionship. There was One who went with them. There were four great things that worried the children of Israel in those forty years.

Number one, **food**. Number two, **water**. Number three, **clothes**. Number four, **health**. They were always concerned about food, water, clothes and health. God did a miracle for them. He fed them with angels' food and every morning, except on the morning of the seventh day, there was an adequate provision. God laid a table for His people and on Saturday He laid it twice so that they could gather for the day of rest. God provides food because He is our companion.

Then they needed **water** the wilderness was a thirsty place but for forty years they had a totally adequate water supply. The sweetest and coolest water you could drink coming from the rock and such a supply that the stream from the rock followed them. They had an ever-fresh supply of water.

Thirdly, they never needed to look for a new suit because their **clothes** grew with them. You say, "Do you believe that preacher?" Surely I believe it. It is nothing to our God. Their clothes, after forty years, were as good as the day they put them on. The shop keepers here would not like it if that happened today. There would be no trade. Their shoes lasted the forty years and their children's garments needed no changing in those forty years. A personal miracle-working, sovereign God took care of their clothes.

He took care of their **health**. It was a miracle in the environment of the wilderness, humanly speaking, for God to preserve something like three million people and keep them from epidemics of diseases. God said, I am Jehovah Rophi, I am the Lord that healeth thee, and the diseases of Egypt will not take their toll upon you.

Let me just for one moment get this into the spiritual realm. In all our wilderness journey and during the past forty years as a denomination we can say that we have had a constant water supply. The water of life has always been available to us as a people. We have been able to slake our thirst at a fountain of the sweetest and most blessed refreshment. We have never lacked any of the Lord's food, the table of God has always been spread. The bread of God has always been available. Thank God the clothes we put on the day we were saved, they have lasted well. The robe of Christ's righteousness never grows old. To have the preparation of the Gospel of peace upon our feet, it never grows old. The garments given to us the day we were born again are the garments that we will wear in heaven, a blood washed robe, whiter than the snow.

Wash me in the blood of the Lamb
And I shall be whiter than snow.

The Lord has preserved us from the diseases of Egypt. Saving us from the sins of the flesh and the sins that mar and scar and stain and destroy the human soul. Why? Remember you have a personal God leading you for forty years, that is companionship. There has never been a time in these forty years that this church has cried to God and God shut His ears to our cry. He has been more willing to answer the prayer than we have been to offer it. He stays with us. He says, lo I am with you always, even unto the end of the age.

FIVE: A PERSONAL GOD LEADING YOU ALL THE WAY

Fifthly, remember you have a personal God leading you all the way. Look at it. *"And thou shalt remember all the way which the Lord thy God led thee."* Put the emphasis on all the way and that is friendship. A friend is a person who goes with you all the way. There is such a thing as fair-weather friends, they are with you when the sun is shining. The Free Presbyterian Church has had many fair-weather friends. They are not with us today, they have not kept the pace and have fallen out by the wayside. But the Lord is the friend all the way. We can look on the dark side and we have had our sicknesses and our disappointments. We have had our hopes shattered. We have walked our way to the graveyard. We have said goodbye to the earthly remains of our nearest and dearest and our hearts have been broken. This morning we long for the touch of the vanished hand and the sound of the voice forever still, but we can say that even that way the Lord was our friend.

> *Standing somewhere in the shadows you'll find Jesus*
> *He's the only One who cares and understands*
> *Standing somewhere in the shadows you will find Him*
> *And you'll know Him by the nailprints in His hands.*

All the way, but we have had days of beauty, we have had days of joy, we have had days of holiness, we have had days of praise, we have had days of refreshment, we have had days of reviving, we have had days of soul winning, we have had days of church openings, we have had days of missionary enterprise, we have had days of sending out the message of this church to now four continents of the whole world. Why? Because God was our friend, that is why. He leads us all the way. With Samuel Rutherford when we cross the dark stream of death and stand on the other side we are going to say

> *I'll bless the hand that guided*
> *I'll bless the heart that planned*

When throned where glory dwelleth
In Immanuel's land.

Remember you have a personal God leading you all the way, that is friendship. A friend that sticketh closer than a brother.

I remember when I was locked up for the first time in Crumlin Road Prison, singing in that cell

What a Friend we have in Jesus
All our sins and griefs to bear
What a privilege to carry
Everything to God in prayer.
Oh what peace we often forfeit
Oh what needless pain we bear
All because we do not carry
Everything to God in prayer.

If I had known, when I stood in that little tin church in Killyleagh Street on 17th March, 1951, what a way God was going to bring me I would have run away. Thank God He has kept us all the way.

SIX: A PERSONAL GOD LEADING YOU TO GREATER THINGS

Lastly, remember you have a personal God leading you to prepare you for greater things. He says that he led them *"to humble thee and to prove thee, to know what was in thine heart, whether thou wouldest keep his commandments."* That is the emphasis on fellowship. You cannot walk with God if you are proud. You need to be humbled. There is one thing that humbles me, that is the kindness of God. I often sit in my study and I think of God's choice in eternity. He did not need to pick me out among the multitudes that no man can number of this earth's teeming millions of all generations, but He did. I did not choose Him, He chose me. That makes me humble.

AMEN AND AMEN!

3 The unfailing compassions *of God*

THE TEXT FOR 1992 is Lamentations 3:22-23, *'It is of the Lord's mercies that we are not consumed, because His compassions fail not. They are new every morning: great is Thy faithfulness.'*

Our text is set in a Book of Sorrows and that is why it shines so brightly. Against the dark backcloth of the sorrows of this Book this promise shines exceedingly. In the Hebrew Bible which is our Old Testament, the Bible of the Hebrews - the Bible of the Jews - there are five Books which are called the five megaliths or scrolls, and these Books are:- the Song of Solomon, the Book of Ruth, the Book of Lamentations, the Book of Ecclesiastes and the Book of Esther.

These five books are always read by the Jews on what is called the Fast of the Ninth Month of their calendar. Their ninth month is our August. They are read because at that time the Jewish nation thinks about the great calamities which have overtaken them. They remember especially the calamity of the return of the spies when they brought a false report and the whole nation had to suffer forty years wandering in the wilderness; the calamity of the destruction of the beautiful temple of Solomon; the calamity of the destruction of the temple that was built under Ezra, Nehemiah and Zerubbabel; the awful slaughter that took place at the destruction of

Jerusalem when Herod's temple was destroyed by the Roman General Titus; the slaughter at Bether of 580,000 Jews by the Roman General Hadrian, and the sorrow when the very site of King David's Zion was put to the plough and not one stone left upon another. They especially read this Book of Lamentations in that connection.

Out of this shadow of sorrow there shines this bright star of glorious Gospel hope. Thomas Watson, one of the most famous of all the Puritans, and a Presbyterian at that, said something quite remarkable. He said he found two great difficulties in all his preaching. Difficulty number one, to make wicked sinners sad. Difficulty number two, to make saints glad. He said he did not know what was the greater of the two difficulties, but he found it very difficult indeed to make the saints glad. It is my task this morning to try and make you glad!. To look at some of your faces, I must tell you, you look mighty sad. So I have some task in hand!

Look at these two texts and you will find that this cluster of gems consists of five bright shining diamonds:-

The first diamond is The Incomparable Source of all Blessings.
Where will we find the source of blessing? *'The Lord's mercies'.*

The second diamond is The Incontestable Safety, *'We are not consumed.'*

We were not consumed yesterday, we will not be consumed today and we will not be consumed tomorrow or ever.

We have got an incontestable safety that no power of Hell can breach or no demon of the pit can destroy.

The third diamond - The Incomprehensible Stream, *'Thy compassions fail not.'*

The compassions of God are flowing onward. There is no limitation to the current of that mighty stream. All who taste its waters are refreshed and bless God, they never thirst again.

The fourth diamond is The Incorruptible Sameness, *'They are new every morning.'*

There is nothing stale or old about God's blessings. They are as fresh as the dew of the morning.

The fifth diamond is The Inconceivable Supply - *'Great is thy faithfulness.'*

There is nothing faithful about us. We are a faithless lot, but how great is the faithfulness of God!

I. THE INCOMPARABLE SOURCE 'IT IS OF THE LORD'S MERCIES'

Let us take the glass, as the jeweller does, and let us put it to our eye and examine these diamonds, these gems.

The Incomparable Source. *'It is of the Lord's mercy,'* No sir! *'It is of the Lord's **mercies**.'*

If you put on your spectacles you will notice that the word 'Lord' in the Authorised Version (and I hope you are not using any other version for the other modern versions we have today are mostly perversions) is in small capitals. What does that mean? In the Hebrew it is the word 'Jehovah' - the I AM - the One Who is not the I was or the I will be, but Who is the I AM - the **Eternal Now** - Unchangeable, Unaging, Immutable. It is His mercies we are talking about.

There is nothing **in** us. There is nothing **of** us. There is nothing **by** us. There is nothing **through** us which merits God's salvation.

God's salvation is by God alone. It is **in** God. It is **of** God. It is **by** God. It is **through** God.

Mercies! What are these mercies? Well, there is the **Mercy of His Wisdom**, He has devised means whereby His banished will not always be expelled from Him.

Add to the Mercy of His Wisdom the **Mercy of His Power**. He reached out and He reached down to the miry pit and, thank God, He reached me. Can you say that? 'He reached out, He reached down and, praise His Name, He reached me.' That is the Mercy of His Power.

What about the **Mercy of His Holiness**? How could filthy sinners, ruined and pocked with sin, ever stand and be accepted and acceptable in the Holy presence of a Thrice Holy God?

The Mercy of his Holiness in finding a way to cleanse us from every spot, every stain, every guilt and every crime and make us fit, not only to be His servants but to be His heirs. That is the Mercy of His Holiness.

What about the **Mercy of His Justice**? In bringing about and appointing a Substitute - Someone to take my place.

Thy mercy, O God, is the theme of my song.
The joy of my heart and the boast of my tongue.
Thy free grace alone from the first to the last
Has won my affections and bound my soul fast.
Thy mercy in Jesus exempts me from hell.
Its glories I'll sing and its wonders I'll tell.
'Twas Jesus my friend when He hung on the tree
He opened a channel of mercy for me!

We can all say, if we are redeemed, a hearty Amen to that! The mercies of God!

II THE INCONTESTABLE SAFETY 'WE ARE NOT CONSUMED'

Let us turn to the second diamond - The Incontestable Safety - *'We are not consumed.'*

Child of God, never forget your weakness. Child of God, never forget the power of the world and the power of the flesh and the power of the devil.

I hear from all over the world how mighty men around us are falling. How godly preachers have been trapped into sin. How churches have been ruined condoning iniquity and how the church of Christ has been turned into a veritable wilderness.

'Let him that standeth take heed lest he fall.' Those words should ring in our ears continually. But I do not need to go through the world in a state of nerves. I do not need to go through the world in a state of sadness. I do not need to go through the world a prey to the enemy. God says, 'We are not consumed.' There is an incontestable safety.

We may walk in the midst of secret and unsuspected dangers. A great preacher once said, 'It is only a small thing that wipes out human life. It may be a whiff of poisonous vapour and that whiff takes the soul from the body. It may be a slip on the street. It may be a car crash. It may be some accident. It may be something very simple, but the simple things can be prophets of doom and hold the assassin's knife in their hand.'

How good God has been in enabling us to live our lives this day, preserving us, healing us, keeping us and watching over us! When we get to Heaven and God shows us the dangers that could have taken us off the face of this earth, when God shows us the minefields that we traversed, when God shows us the dangerous path that our feet tread successfully by his grace, we will then know that it was of the Lord's mercies that we were not consumed.

If simple things can bring physical death, simple things can also bring spiritual death to the life of the believer. Little things - the little foxes that spoil the vines for the vines have tender grapes.

Oh how shall we continue in the path? How shall we persevere in holiness and in goodness and in truth? Left to ourselves we will fall and end our Christian race in disaster, but with the Lord's mercies we shall not be consumed.

> *'Tell of His wondrous faithfulness,*
> *And sound His power abroad,*
> *Sing of the promise of His grace,*
> *And the performing God.'*

It is God who will keep us! Let us put our faith in this incontestable safety, 'It is of the Lord's mercies that we are not consumed.' As one has said, 'You will never fall if you are face downwards on the Rock.' And you never will. So get face downwards on the Rock. Be very sure your anchor holds and grips the solid Rock, and that Rock is Jesus!

III THE INCOMPREHENSIBLE STREAM
'THY COMPASSIONS FAIL NOT.'

Open your Bible at Psalm 103. We were singing out of this great Psalm today. In it we have those marvellous words:-

'The Lord is merciful, and gracious, slow to anger, and plenteous in mercy. He will not always chide; neither will He keep His anger for ever. He hath not dealt with us after our sins; nor rewarded us according to our

*iniqui*ties. *For as the heaven is high above the earth, so great is His mercy toward them that fear Him. As far as the east is from the west, so far hath he removed our transgressions from us. Like as a father pitieth his children, so the Lord pitieth them that fear Him. For He knoweth our frame; He remembereth that we are dust.'*

> *My soul repeats His praise,*
> *Whose mercies are so great*
> *Whose anger is so slow to rise,*
> *So ready to abate.*
>
> *High as the heavens are raised*
> *Above the ground we tread,*
> *So far the riches of His grace*
> *Our highest thoughts exceed.*
>
> *God will not always chide*
> *And where His strokes are felt,*
> *His strokes are fewer than our crimes*
> *And lighter than our guilt.*
>
> *His power subdues our sins,*
> *And His forgiving love,*
> *Far as the east is from the west,*
> *Does all our guilt remove.*

'*Thy compassion*'? No! '*Thy compassions*' (plural) 'fail not.' He cannot fail for He is God! Unfailing compassions!

There may be a situation in 1992 when no man will have compassion on you; when no Christian brother will have pity for you, circumstances so terrible that friends once depended on by you will fail. There is something that will not fail and that is God's compassions. When you are shut up, and like David, a sparrow alone on the housetop in bitter sorrow and terrible isolation, let me give you this text. In such circumstances you will be able to cry out, *'Thy compassions fail not.'* Jesus never fails. Heaven and earth may pass away, but Jesus never fails.

V THE INCORRUPTIBLE SAMENESS
'THEY ARE NEW EVERY MORNING.'

Let us turn to the fourth diamond - The Incorruptible Sameness - *'They are new every morning.'*

The compassions of God are never stale. They are always fresh. Why? Because they flow from the well of the heart of the Unchanging God. God's heart knows no changes. God had surely a tender heart when He sent His Son to die for you. He surely had a tender heart when He put His Son to the sword that you might be delivered from wrath to come. He surely had a tender heart when He pressed to the lips of His Son that dreadful cup and commanded Him to drink it to the dregs. He surely had a tender heart when He reached out after you in your sin and in your rebellion and in your stupidity and obstinacy and broke your heart by the power of the Spirit and drew you to salvation and to grace.

Well, His heart is as tender to you today as when He gave His Son to die for you. It is as tender to you today as when Christ hung upon that Cross of shame and the Father put Him to the sword. It is as tender to you today as when He drew you, that sweet and blessed happy day, to Himself. God does not change. 'They are new every morning.' God's compassions are tender compassions for they partake of God's Unageingness. They are undimmed because they partake of God's Brightness. They are unwaning because they partake of God's Sameness.

Oh, the tenderness, the unchangeableness, the unageingness, the brightness and the sameness of God's compassions. Here is a pillow that you can always lay a weary head upon. Here is a place where you can always find succour. Here is a place that no circumstance is so terrible or horrendous that the soul cannot find sweet comfort there.

> *Oh to lie forever here,*
> *Doubt and care and self resign*
> *While He whispers in my ear,*
> *I am His and He is mine.*

Why does the prophet talk about these compassions being new every morning? Because the only thing in nature that keeps regularity and constancy is the return of the day. We do not know when the rain will come or the rain will go. We do not know when the wind will blow and when the wind will be stilled. Springtime can come early or late. Wintertime can come early or late. Summertime can come early or late. Autumntime can come early or late, but there is one thing that comes with constancy and regularity and it is the new day. When the new day comes it wears the mantle of the dew of the morning, and every day is a fresh day, every day is a bedewed day and every day is a new day.

That is like the compassions of God, they come to us with the dew of the morning upon them. How sweet to taste this nectar! How sweet to partake of this honey! How sweet to sit at this festal feast that God has provided for us! *'Thy compassions fail not, they are new every morning.'*

Make sure you draw your seat to the table every morning. make sure, before you face the difficulties and the struggles and the trials and the battles of a new day, make sure you get your vitamins - divine vitamins - the necessary vitamins for the strengthening of your soul. *'Man cannot live by bread alone, but by every Word that proceedeth out of the mouth of God.'*

V   THE INCONCEIVABLE SUPPLY
'GREAT IS THY FAITHFULNESS.'

Let us look at the fifth diamond - the Inconceivable Supply - *'Great is Thy faithfulness.'* Our need is great but the supply is greater than all our need. Our need is constant but this great supply flows on like a mighty river.

> *'Grace is flowing like a river,*
> *Millions there have been supplied,*
> *Still it flows as fresh as ever*
> *From the Saviour's wounded side.'*

Inconceivable supply!

The brook Cherith that supplied old Elijah with drink, dried up, but this brook never dries up.

This brook is like the barrel of meal that cannot waste and the cruse of oil that cannot fail.

Adam partook of its waters and he cried out, *'Great is Thy faithfulness.'* An innumerable company of the saints of all Ages have come to this life-giving stream and they have partaken of this inconceivable supply, and they have all cried out, *'Great is Thy faithfulness.'* This is the shout of the saints of God, 'Great is Thy faithfulness.' This is the testimony of the angels of God, *'Great is Thy faithfulness.'* This is the doxology of all creation, *'Great is Thy faithfulness.'* This is the unceasing tribute of Ages past, of the Age that now is and of the Ages yet to come, *'Great is Thy faithfulness.'* God is faithful Who promised, He also will do it!

Dr. John Brown, the famous Scottish theologian, visited an old dying saint. He thought he would test her as she neared the river, so he said, 'Janet, what would you think that after all God had done for you He allowed you to drop into hell?' Janet, unperturbed, looked at Dr. Brown and said in her broad Scottish accent, 'E'en as He likes but He'll lose more than I will.' What did she mean? She said if God let her drop into hell He would lose His Godhead. He would lose His integrity. He would lose His honesty. He would lose His faithfulness. He would lose everything that made Him God. 'He will lose more than I would.'

What a testimony! God cannot die. God cannot lie. God is faithful. *'Great is Thy faithfulness.'*

No doubt you and I this year will come under the rod of affliction, for we are born to affliction as the sparks fly upwards.

It was old Charles Simeon who said, 'When the saint is in affliction he takes four views. One, he notices the lightness of the affliction in comparison to what he deserves. Our light affliction is but for a moment. He takes into consideration the multitude of God's mercies still continued to him, even though he is afflicted. He views the unchangeableness of God under all dispensations, and he discovers the beauty of a religion that brings suffering, for if we suffer with Him we shall also be glorified together.'

'Great is Thy faithfulness.'

There are some with us today and this time next year they will not be with us. There were some with us last year at our first Lord's Day service and they are not with us today. They have gone in to see the King in His beauty.

When we reach those pearl hung gates and golden streets we will have the same testimony, *'Great is Thy faithfulness.'* When ten million trillion years of the vast eternity are gone, if you meet me in Glory Square I will say, *'Great is His faithfulness.'* This is the unending Motto of the people of God. Let us make it ours in the coming days of this year, for Jesus' Sake.

AMEN & AMEN

4 God perfecting
His people

OUR MOTTO TEXT FOR 1993 is Psalm 138:7-8 *"Though I walk in the midst of trouble, thou wilt revive me: thou shalt stretch forth thine hand against the wrath of mine enemies, and thy right hand shall save me. The Lord will perfect that which concerneth me: thy mercy O Lord, endureth for ever: forsake not the works of thine own hands."*

David, in this ending to the Psalm, highlights the difficulties, the oppositions, the obstacles and the antagonism that he has to face as he walks through this earthly pilgrimage.

You will notice, first of all, he has to face adversity. He is in the midst of trouble. Adverse circumstances, adverse conditions surround him, he is in the midst of adversity. As long as you live in this world, child of God, you will be in the midst of adversity.

Then secondly, you will notice he highlights the hostility. Oh he has not only adversity but he has bitter, bitter poisonous hostility released upon him and he describes it as *'the wrath of thine enemies'*. As the child of God goes on the pilgrim's progress he is not only in the midst of adversity but he is in the midst of hostility, the wrath of his enemies will be continually released upon him. He will be the target and the object of hostility of all the antichrist forces in all the world. He is targeted by hell, by the Devil, by the world, by the flesh and by all that is in the world and all that is in hell and in the heart of the malignant Satan himself.

Thirdly, he is face to face with extremity. He is at wit's end corner and the circumstances are the same every day. There is adversity today, adversity tomorrow, adversity the week after, the month after, the year after. He says to himself, I am glad God's mercy is forever. Thank God there will be a day when the extremity of opposition will finish but God's mercy will never finish because God's mercy is forever.

REVIVAL IN ADVERSITY

These two verses give to the saints of God the never-failing promise of their faithful God. First of all we read, *"Though I walk in the midst of trouble, thou wilt revive me"*. Here is the promise of revival in adversity.

You will notice that all three parts of these two verses are based upon what God does. If you are depending in life upon what you are going to do you are going to utterly fail. If you are depending on your own strength to fight the battle, to win the victory and to get through triumphantly you are going to be completely and totally and absolutely disillusioned and disappointed and overthrown. You notice the Psalmist bases his confidence, his faith, his hope upon the will and work of God.

Look at the first section, *"thou wilt revive me"*. Look at the second section, *"thou shalt stretch forth thy hand."* Look at verse eight *"the Lord will perfect that which concerneth me."* The covenant of grace is a covenant of the "I will's" of God. It is not a covenant of what thou shalt do. It is a covenant of what God says He will do. That is the difference between law and grace. Law makes demands but grace gives the blessing. We don't get to heaven by our own strength or our own zeal or our own enthusiasm or dedication. We get to heaven by the grace of God alone and the trouble today is that many who have begun in the spirit are trying to perfect themselves in the flesh and that is why there is so much sin in the church and backsliding among believers.

I want you to notice something about this. The Psalmist is not on the edge of trouble, notice that. The believer is never on the edge of trouble. He is not just a little way into these troubles. He is in the midst of trouble. There is trouble to the right of him, trouble to the left of him, trouble before him, behind him, beneath him and above him. He is surrounded with trouble. He is overwhelmed with trouble.

In my private reading this morning I was reading Psalm 3, If you turn to it you will find here what the Psalmist was experiencing, *"Lord how have they increased that trouble me, many are they that rise up against me, many they be which say of my soul there is no help for him in God."* In the midst of trouble. Thank God, in the midst of trouble, trouble that has squeezed the very life blood out of the Psalmist. Trouble that has left him like the man on the road to Jericho, covered with wounds and lying half dead by the wayside. What does he say? He says there is a promise of revival in adversity, *"thou wilt revive me"*. That word is thou wilt give me life. Thou wilt give me thy breath. Thou wilt give me an enlivening, a quickening, a resurrection. This is what the church of Jesus Christ needs. God can give us life out of the trouble. God can give us life in the midst of the trouble and God can give us life through the trouble. Sometimes it is a good thing for God to give you the whip. Sometimes it is a good thing for God to bring chastisement to you. Sometimes it is a good thing to be scourged by God. The Psalmist said, *"Before I was afflicted I went astray."*

Dear child of God, here we have the promise of revival in adversity. If you are a Christian and you have never read John Bunyan's Pilgrim's Progress go and buy yourself a copy and read it in 1993. When you read it you will realise what you missed. In the second part where Christiana and her children are headed for the celestial city a man appears who is called Valiant for the Truth. Mr Valiant for the Truth was set upon by three thieves. He drew his sword and he struggled and he battled and he fought well and fought hard until he was drenched with blood from head to toe. Then another great character Mr Great Heart came along and the foes fled away. Mr Valiant for the Truth said, "I am bleeding, I am exhausted, life seems to be drained from me." Great Heart washed his wounds and refreshed him from the bottle of reviving which he carried.

You will find that the Psalmist goes on and he says *"thou shalt stretch forth thine hand against the wrath of mine enemies and thy right hand shall save me."* Here is the promise of contrival in hostility.

CONTRIVAL IN HOSTILITY

The Lord contrives in the miracle of His providence to make all things work together for good to them that love God, to them who are called according to His purpose. If you turn over to Psalm 27, the Psalmist looks around him and he is amazed about what is happening. *"When the wicked, even mine enemies and my foes, came upon me to eat up my flesh, they stumbled and fell. The Lord is my light and my salvation; whom shall I fear? the Lord is the strength of my life; of whom shall I be afraid? Though an host should encamp against me my heart shall not fear: though war should rise against me, in this will I be confident."* You will notice here that there is a right-handed deliverance for the children of God. In this text you will find that this contrival on the part of God to deliver His child, is all of the Lord's doing. You can't face the wrath of the enemy. You can't face the battle with the devil and win that battle. He will throw you every time. Greater men than you have fought with Satan. Eve, the innocent, sinless woman in the paradise of God did not win the battle over Satan, and you cannot win the battle over Satan but thank God there is a strong right hand that can win the battle over the devil.

Who can fight the flesh? David, a man after God's own heart, fell into the vile black hellish shameful pit of adultery. The man that wrote this very Psalm became a liar, an adulterer and a murderer. You cannot fight the flesh and win the battle.

Samson, the strongest man that ever lived. Solomon, the wisest man that ever lived, tried to fight the world and the world threw them both and trod them like worms beneath the world's feet. Ah, but there is One, the great I AM, the Prince Immanuel, the King of kings, the Lord of lords, the Lion of the tribe of Judah, and He has a right handed deliverance for us but it is His doing. He must do it.

You will notice it is by God's strength. The right hand. He shall stretch forth His hand. The right hand in the Bible is an interesting hand. It means the hand that is seen. It is always the seen hand. It is like the right arm. *"Thou shalt make bare thine arm."* That was the way they declared war in those days. The chief brought his armed forces together and sitting on his horse he took his sleeve and rolled it up until his right hand was bare, then he lifted it on high, it was a signal of war. God has made bare His strong right arm on behalf of His people. It is the Lord's strength alone that can bring us through this year and the Lord has already the plan. He has already contrived the way. Do you remember the old woman of Tekoah? She said, *"We are as water spilt upon the ground which cannot be gathered up. But God has devised means whereby His banished be not always expelled from Him."* God has already the means devised and we should look with joy and faith to the making bare of God's right hand. That will deal with the wrath of the enemy. That will deal with the forces of the enemy.

Oh that we might see the hand of the Lord's doing and the might of God's strength intervening. What does this country need? It needs an intervention of God. Only God can turn the tide. Only God can save us. Here we have the promise, the promise of revival in adversity and contrival in hostility and you can sing Psalm 27 in the darkest day. *"Of whom shall I be afraid, though an host encamp against me, my heart shall not fear: though wars should rise against me, in this will I be confident."* Confident of what? The strong right hand of God.

Let us turn to the last verse, verse eight. Here it says, *"The Lord will perfect that which concerneth me: thy mercy, O Lord, endureth for ever: forsake not the works of thine own hands."* Notice the difference. For the enemy it is the right hand but for God's children we are the work of both His hands. You have to get the meaning of that by going to the Song of Solomon. "His left hand is under my head. His right hand doth embrace me." The left hand in the Bible is the secret hand of God. You don't see it. It is behind you, it is under your head. You don't know how God has planned all things out but He has planned all things out for the glory of His name. Sometimes circumstances have come to me in life and I have thought it is the end, for *"no chastening for the present is joyous but grievous but afterwards it yieldeth the peaceable fruit of righteousness."* When I was first imprisoned in 1966 people thought it was the end of the world and Terence O'Neill declared that Paisleyism was dead. I did three months in the Crumlin Road and the first morning I preached in the old church, that hand gave the right hand of fellowship to 200 new members. 200 new members. One of my elders said to me, "You should have stayed in jail six months." I said, "Friend, you can do the other three months, I am quite happy to be out."

THE PRAYER OF SURVIVAL

Let me say something to you friend, we need the intervention of the God who is going to make us survive. There is not only revival in this text and contrival in this text, there is survival in this text. The Christian survives. You will notice that there is the prayer of survival here. He says *"Forsake not the work of thine own hands."* He says I am a child of God, I am your responsibility, Father take care of me, Lord Jesus look after me, blessed Holy Spirit empower me. That is the prayer that comes from the heart. Where do you go in trouble? To your neighbour? To your friends? To your preacher? You should run to God when you are in trouble. The first thing that I do when I am in trouble is I pray. I don't care where I am or whose company I am in, I say we will pray. That is what you do, you pray.

THE PROSPECT OF SURVIVAL

You remember Pilgrim going through the valley of humiliation and Apollyon had him defeated. He dropped his sword and was about to be finished when he thought of that invincible weapon of prayer - and he prayed and the circumstances changed. He got hold of the sword again and slew Apollyon who went off screaming over his wounds. Oh my friend there is a prayer for survival. Are we offering that prayer every day? Are we crying to God for the survival of the church in this evil day? The Psalmist was at wit's end corner. There is a place to do something at wit's end corner, it is to offer the prayer of survival. You will notice that there is not only the fervent prayer of survival here but there is the full prospect of survival. We will survive - the Lord will complete that which concerneth me.

> *"The work which His goodness began,*
> *The arm of His strength will complete.*
> *His promise is yea and amen,*
> *And never was forfeited yet.*
> *Yes, I to the end shall endure,*
> *As sure as the earnest is given,*
> *More happy but not more secure,*
> *Than glorified with Him in heaven."*

He is going to complete what He has begun. Every day the Christian says, "The best is yet to be and the end is not yet, praise the Lord."

Here we have the prospect, the full prospect of survival. What a great thing it will be when God brings to perfection what He has started. That is why the Christian should be looking every day for a mighty stirring of the blessed Holy Spirit. Can these dry bones live? Yes sir, they can, when the Spirit of God comes.

THE PILLAR OF SURVIVAL

Notice thirdly, there is a firm pillar of survival here. What does he rest on? He rests on this, *"thy mercy O Lord endureth for ever"*. That is the pillar that you lean on, the pillar of God's mercy, and it is from everlasting to everlasting.

> *"Before the hills in order stood,*
> *Or earth received her frame.*
> *From everlasting thou art God*
> *To endless years the same.*

The mercy of God is the same. That day you knelt at the cross a broken, weak hell-deserving wretch, knowing the full vengeance of God on sin and you cried for mercy. Something happened at the cross. What happened? The mercy of God - God saved you. His mercy is the same today as it was on the day of your first birthday. The same today.

> *Yesterday, today, forever*
> *Jesus is the same.*
> *All may change but Jesus never*
> *Glory to His Name.*

This promise is a wonderful promise. These promises rest on God's quickening power, God's intervening power, God's saving power, God's perfecting power, God's merciful power, God's eternal power and God's immutable power.

There is no fear of this pillar breaking. There is no fear of this foundation crumbling. There is no fear of this building ever toppling. It will stand steadfast for ever. Old Abraham looked for a city, which had foundation, whose builder and maker is God.

Dear child of God, today go home, with this promise embedded in your soul, the promise of revival in adversity, contrival in hostility and survival in extremity in Jesus' name.

Father, write thy truth upon every heart and give the joy of faith in every child of God's being today. For unsaved ones here who are strangers to God's grace save them, help them to cry out to God for salvation and life for Jesus's sake.

AMEN AND AMEN

5 Seven diamonds in the *believer's love ring*

OUR MOTTO TEXT FOR 1994 can be found in Psalm 91: 14-16, *"Because he hath set his love upon me, therefore will I deliver him: I will set him on high, because he hath known my name. He shall call upon me, and I will answer him: I will be with him in trouble; I will deliver him, and honour him. With long life will I satisfy him, and shew him my salvation."*

Every year I take a text of Scripture and my Church and I make it our Motto Text for the year.

How appropriate and practical these motto texts become. Last year we had a most appropriate text, just the very promise of power we required for the dark valleys and conflicts of the year just gone. Psalm 137: 7-8 *"Though I walk in the midst of trouble, thou wilt revive me: thou shalt stretch forth thine hand against the wrath of mine enemies, and thy right hand shall save me. The Lord will perfect that which concerneth me: thy mercy, O Lord, endureth for ever: forsake not the works of thine own hands."*

This year I am taking the above text. It was suggested to me in a small volume called *"Beulah Land"* written by a great friend of Spurgeon, Dr. T.L. Culyer.

Here is a love-ring we can wear each day of 1994. Its diamonds will never lose their sparkle. It is the gift for all who set their love on God.

*Oh, set not your love on the **world** this year for it will **deceive** you.*
*Oh, set not you love on the **flesh** this year for it will **defile** you.*
*Oh, set not you love on the **devil** this year for he will **destroy** you.*
*Oh, set not you love on your **companions** for they will **disappoint** you.*

Oh, set your love on the Saviour and on His Father and your Father and His Spirit and your spirit.

The reason for the giving of this ring is, you are setting your love upon Him. How many believers this year will not be able to wear this love-ring? It will be strangely and sadly absent from their finger because they are wedded to other loves.

Love strong as death, nay stronger,
Love mightier than the grave;
Broad as the earth, and longer
Than ocean's wider wave.

To gladder days from saddest night,
From deepest shame to glory bright,
From depths of death to life's fair light,
From darkness to the joy of light.

- Horatius Bonar

Having tasted that love may ours be consistently the cry of the Apostle of Love, *"We love Him because He first loved us."* John 4: 19

Thomas Watson, the Presbyterian Puritan was right, *"Love is the only thing in which we can retaliate with God ... We must not give Him word for word but love for love."*

Oh the *"therefore's"* of God. They are as strong and sure as God Himself. *"Therefore"* He says, *"I will"*.

When God says, *"I will"* it is done. For *"He spake and it was done, He commanded and it stood fast."* Psalm 33:9.

But, remember He only speaks and commands those who set their love upon Him. Oh, knit my soul to thy soul of love Lord Jesus, Thou Greater David, as Jonathan's soul was knit to the lesser David's soul. 1 Samuel 18: 1.

I. THE FIRST DIAMOND IN THE BELIEVER'S LOVE-RING IS THE DIAMOND OF GOD'S POWER - "I WILL DELIVER HIM"

Only Christ's power can deliver us from Satan, self and sin.

We come into the world strangled by this threefold cord. We are born in subjection to Satan and self and sin.

Our path-way is a veritable minefield. We will never negotiate it. We are doomed.

Satan desired to have Peter but the Lord prayed for Peter and delivered him. On the day of Pentecost Peter wore the love-ring and the diamond sparkled forth this message, *"I will deliver thee."*

Sin tried to have Joseph but the Lord was with Joseph and delivered him and the day he stood before Pharaoh he wore the love-ring and the diamond sparkled forth this message, *"I will deliver thee."*

Self tried to have David but the Lord did not forsake him and when he came forth chastened and forgiven he wore the love-ring and the diamond sparkled, *"I will deliver thee."*

Christ delivered us from the penalty of our sin the day we were **justified** and on the basis of His blood payment we were freed. There is therefore for us in Christ - **"No Condemnation"**. But note carefully the word. There is therefore **now** no condemnation. Romans 8:1.

It is true in the **now** of today. It is true in the **now** of tomorrow. It is true in the **now** of eternity. What a blessed assurance this is. Rare old Thomas Brooks the Puritan exclaimed, *"Assurance is glory in the bud, it is the suburbs of paradise".*

Christ is delivering us from the power of sin as He **sanctifies** us. On the basis that on the cross He died to bring in the charter of liberty, "Sin shall not have dominion over you" Romans 6: 14, thus robbing our old man of the power to control us. Whom Christ sets free is free indeed. *I will deliver thee.*

What a blessed assurance this is but always keep in mind what Thomas Fuller the rare and ancient historian wrote, *"Assurance has a narrow throat, and may be choked with a small sin."*

Christ will deliver us from the presence of sin when He **glorifies** us. Someday final deliverance will be ours. On the resurrection advent morning we will wear this love-ring and the sparkling first diamond will declare to all the eternal message from God's own lips *"I will deliver you"*.

Thomas Adams, in many ways the first Adam of the Puritans, said, *"Heaven begins where sin ends."*

II THE SECOND DIAMOND IN THE BELIEVER'S LOVE-RING IS THE DIAMOND OF GOD'S PRESERVATION - "I WILL SET HIM ON HIGH"

High above the world, the flesh and the devil, and all his and our enemies, the Lord is a **sure** refuge. No potency can ever disintegrate this Rock. It is sure. The Lord is a **safe** refuge. What safety is in Christ! The saints of all ages found safety in Him. None of them ever perished, for none can pluck out of the Saviour's hand or the Father's hand. The Lord is a **sweet** refuge. How sweet it is to be in the cleft of the Rock of Ages. Here is the Sweetest of all sweets, the Paradise of all paradises, the Heaven of all heavens, the Rest of all rests.

The fight is on; arise, ye soldiers
brave and true!
Jehovah leads and victory will assure;
Go, buckle on the armour God has
given you,
And in His strength unto the end endure.

The fight is on, O Christian soldier,
And face to face in stern array,
With armour gleaming and colours streaming,
The right and wrong engage today!

The fight is on, but be not weary:
Be strong, and in His might hold fast;
If God be for us, His banner o'er us,
We'll sing the victor's song at last.

As we walk the battlements of the Eternal Rock of Ages and mark her bulwarks and consider her palaces let us wear this love-ring and let it's second diamond sparkle so as to dazzle the faces of all our foes. *I will set him on high.*

III. THE THIRD DIAMOND IN THE BELIEVER'S LOVE-RING IS THE DIAMOND OF GOD'S PLEASURE - "I WILL ANSWER HIM"

Ah, here is the best possible two-way traffic, our prayers going up, His answers coming down. Alas, our prayers are sluggish. They never get out of first gear. Hallelujah, His answers are swift, they are always in overdrive. They come so quickly they past the prayers on the way up. Glory to our God.

"And it shall come to pass that before they call, I will answer; and while they are yet speaking, I will hear." Isaiah 65: 24

God summonses us to prayer but prayer summonses God to answer.

"I will answer him." There's not a doubt about that.

"Fear not, little flock: for it is your Father's good pleasure to give you the kingdom." Luke 12: 32

The answer is on the way. Let this sparkling diamond light the path of prayer for us each day.

IV. THE FOURTH DIAMOND IN THE BELIEVER'S LOVE-RING IS THE DIAMOND OF GOD'S PRESENCE - "I WILL BE WITH HIM IN TROUBLE"

All men and women, whether God's children or Satan's are born into trouble as the sparks fly upward. Job 5: 7.

The first utterance from all babies' lips is one of need. The Christian however is specially appointed unto trouble.

It is by the fire that true metal is tested. So it is by the fiery trials that the true mettle of men and women are tested.

We must pass the fire test of trouble in time. There is no escape from the burning fiery furnace.

God chooses His people in the furnace of affliction. But God is with His people in the flame. A fourth person was seen in the furnace, One like the Son of God. *"I will be with thee in trouble."*

Yes we are beaten to be made better. We are burned in order to be blessed. We are purged in order to be pure. We are polished in order to be pleasing. The cut of the rod is in order to the comfort of the staff. Only the dross burns in the flame, our durability comes forth unscathed. As the sea and the whale brought Jonah safe to land so do the storms and sufferings of life.

Spurgeon was right, *"There are no crown wearers in heaven that were not cross-bearers here below."*

But in trouble, the Saviour is with us. His sweet presence ever abides. The staff comforts for it protects, the Master's hand is right beside me.

I picked up an old tattered hymn book yesterday and read these words. They are most appropriate.

> *There are days so dark that I seek in vain*
> *For the face of my Friend Divine;*
> *But tho' darkness hide,*
> *He is there to guide,*
> *By the touch of His hand on mine.*
>
> *Oh, the touch of His hand on mine,*
> *Oh, the touch of His hand on mine!*
> *There is grace and pow'r, in the trying hour,*
> *In the touch of His hand on mine.*
>
> *There are times, when tired of the toilsome road,*
> *That for ways of the world I pine;*
> *But He draws me back to the upward track,*
> *By the touch of His hand on mine.*
>
> *When the way is dim, I cannot see*
> *Thro' the midst of His wise design,*
> *How my glad heart yearns and my faith returns*
> *By the touch of His hand on mine.*

In the last sad hour, as I stand alone
Where the powers of death combine,
While the dark waves roll He will guide my soul
By the touch of His hand on mine.

Let this diamond sparkle as you gaze upon, it for it will cut you a way even through steel itself and like the star lead you to where the Lord Jesus is. *I will be with him in trouble.*

V. THE FIFTH DIAMOND IN THE BELIEVER'S LOVE-RING IS THE DIAMOND OF GOD'S PROMOTION - "I WILL HONOUR HIM"

The honours of men are trifles. The honours of God are tremendous. Christ honours His people with **His Friendship**. He says so lovingly *"Ye are my friends"*.

Listen to these sweet and holy words from the lips of God Incarnate.

"Greater love hath no man than this, that a man lay down his life for his friends. Ye are my friends, if ye do whatsoever I command you. Henceforth I call you not servants; for the servant knoweth not what his lord doeth: but I have called you friends: for all things that I have heard of my Father I have made known unto you." John 15: 13-15

We share His secrets. We are friends of Jesus.

Christ honours His people with His Ownership. He will never deny is. Hear these blessed words. *"And they shall be mine, saith the Lord of hosts, in that day when I make up my jewels; and I will spare them, as a man spareth his own son that serveth him."* Malachi 3: 17 *"Whosoever therefore shall confess me before men, him will I confess also before my Father which is in heaven."* Matthew 10: 32.

Thine, Thine, Thine,
I know I am Thine,
Saviour dear Saviour,
I know I am Thine.

Christ honours His people with **His throneship.**

We are heirs of God. We are also joint heirs with Christ. He cannot inherit without us. We are going to share His Father's throne with Him.

Hear this trumpet announcement!

Be silent all devils of perdition!

Be silent all angels of paradise!

Be silent all damned spirits!

Be silent all saved spirits!

Be silent all ye dwellers on the earth!

Be silent all ye dwellers in the heavens!

Christ has spoken.

"To him that overcometh will I grant to sit with me in my throne, even as I also overcame, and am set down with my Father in his throne" Revelation 3: 21

Let the sparkle of this diamond glitter invitingly every day of 1994.

VI. THE SIXTH DIAMOND IN THE BELIEVER'S LOVE-RING IS THE DIAMOND OF GOD'S PROVISION - "I WILL SATISFY HIM"

Length of days and provision for every day was in the Old Testament the special evidence of God's favour.

But "long life" goes far far broader than any calendar. On earth God gives us the quality of living and in heaven God gives us the quantity of living - that is what everlasting life is.

Christ taught us a great truth which many Christians have never yet learned.

"And He said unto them, Take heed, and beware of covetousness: for a man's life consisteth not in the abundance of the things which he possesseth." Luke 12: 15

Christ came that we might have true life, God's life, everlasting life and life more abundantly. John 10: 10.

This long life enables the believer to take the long look at life and causes him like Joshua to ask for a long day that he might fight the battles of the Lord. He cries for the sun of his day of service to stand still, so that he can have time to glorify his Lord and have much fruit and many trophies to lay at the Saviour's feet. He only wants the necessities of life so that his service for Christ will not be hindered. He is wise like Solomon to this end.

"Two things have I required of thee; deny me them not before I die. Remove far from me vanity and lies: give me neither poverty nor riches; feed me with food convenient for me: Lest I be full and deny thee, and say, Who is the Lord? or lest I be poor, and steal, and take the name of my God in vain." Proverbs 30: 7-9

For the true Christian, to live is Christ and to die is gain. He is satisfied with Christ now, he will be satisfied when he awakes in Christ's likeness. Psalm 17: 15

Look upon this diamond and let it light your path with contentment all the days of your life.

David read its gleaming message and sang,

Goodness and mercy all my life
Shall surely follow me
And in God's house for evermore
My dwelling place shall be.

VII THE SEVENTH DIAMOND IN THE BELIEVER'S LOVE-RING IS THE DIAMOND OF GOD'S PRESENTATION - "I WILL SHEW HIM MY SALVATION"

Who is God's Salvation? Why, Christ is God's Salvation.

When old man Simeon took up in his arms God Incarnate in human form, a tiny babe, he cried out *"Mine eyes have seen thy Salvation"* Luke 2: 30. Others saw a child ,Simeon saw God's Salvation. His eyes were open to behold what Habakkuk rejoiced about, the revelation, the shewing, of God's Salvation.

"Although the fig tree shall not blossom, neither shall fruit be in the vines; the labour of the olive shall fail, and the fields shall yield no meat; the flock shall be cut off from the fold, and there shall be no herd in the stalls: **Yet I will rejoice in the Lord, I will joy in the God of my salvation.** *The Lord God is my strength, and he will make my feet like hinds' feet, and he will*

make me to walk upon mine high places. To the chief singer on my stringed instruments." Habakkuk 3: 17-19.

Let us pray David's prayer, *"Say unto my soul I am thy salvation."* Psalm 35: 3.

Yes, we have seen God's Salvation in time, in regeneration, in sanctification and in salvation but one day we shall see Him as He is, and wonder of wonder, we shall be like Him.

Here is a diamond which sparkles from the believer's love-ring. *"I will shew him my salvation."*

I was thinking this week of my beloved friend, and gracious fellow soldier and preaching colleague Pastor Willie Mullan as I saw again a video which I presented many years ago with him. One day he wrote these words. They go to the tune of Londonderry Air, *O Danny Boy.*

> *"There is a name*
> *So high above all other names*
> *That lovely name*
> *So sweet, so dear to me.*
> *The Rose of Sharon, Lily of the Valley,*
> *The King of kings and Lord of lords is He.*
> *Lord Jesus Christ,*
> *The Lamb of God for ever.*
> *The Prince of Peace*
> *And Saviour, let me tell;*
> *The Mighty God,*
> *The Everlasting Father,*
> *The Wonderful, The Counsellor, Emmanuel.*
>
> *This precious name*
> *Adored by men and angels,*
> *The Lord of Glory,*
> *Shepherd of the sheep,*
> *The First and Last, Beginner of creation,*
> *The Man of Sorrows, Jesus, see Him weep.*

The Holy One,
The Son of God eternal,
Our Great High Priest
And Advocate as well,
And Israel's King,
Messiah, Prince and Ruler,
The Righteous Judge,
My Lord, my God, Emmanuel".

Willie has seen the One of whom he wrote so beautifully and preached so powerfully and with the diamond love-ring on our finger we are on the way to see Him too.

Dear unsaved one, you must see Him by the eye of faith in time if you are going to see Him in eternity in glory. *"Behold the Lamb of God which taketh away the sin of the world."* John 1: 29 **Look to the Saviour now and there you will live with Him forever.**

AMEN AND AMEN!

6 Abounding unto
every good work

WE ARE TURNING IN our Bible to the ninth chapter of II Corinthians. The Motto that I have chosen for 1995 is the eighth verse of the ninth chapter of II Corinthians: *"And God is able to make all grace abound toward you; that ye, always having all sufficiency in all things, may abound to every good work."*

INTRODUCTION - PRESSURE

Immense pressures are upon us all in these eventful days. Sometimes we are forced to exclaim, as Paul did in the first chapter he wrote to the Corinthian church, when he said he was pressed out of measure, above strength, insomuch he despaired of life itself. Individual pressures are upon us all; they relate to our persons, our minds, our bodies, and our inmost souls. They are like the taskmasters of Egypt. They come down with a cruel cutting lash upon us, and we are brought very low in heart, spirit and mind. Then there are family pressures upon us. Anxiety for our homes, anxiety for our offspring, anxiety about their spiritual wellbeing and their eternity. And those pressures on Christian parents increase mightily in these days of increasing apostasy and in the rising tide of sin and wicked temptations on every hand. Then there are social pressures upon us - the circumstances, the responsibilities we have in this society of ours, and upon us also are the pressures of our work, the pressures of our employment, the pressures that bring strain and frustration in our daily workload and our daily occupation.

Then we have our church pressures. We despair at our lack of zeal for the Lord of hosts. We are pressed down by the fact that our spiritual life is under exceeding strain. Circumstances crowd out God, crowd out Christ, and crowd out our times of prayer and our times of Bible reading, and we have nerve-wearing problems as a result of all these pressures. Many of God's people are worried and carry an extreme pressure of worry in mind and in heart.

You will remember Naomi. She was under pressure. The word "Naomi" means "Pleasant one", but she was no longer a pleasant one. When she returned to her home, instead of happiness there was despair. Instead of hope there was hopelessness, and she said, "Call me not Naomi, call me Mara, for I am bitter. Out from the depths I cry to Thee." And so she cried out of the depths to God.

The text I have chosen this year is God's remedy for worry, strain, pressure. Whether it be family worry, domestic worry, personal worry, or worry about business, or church, or society. What a text it is! It presents us with three views of God. Number one, "God is" - the Actuality of God. Number two, "God is able" - the Ability of God. Number three, "God is able to make" - the Activity of God.

For a few minutes this morning I want to dwell upon this wonderful topic of God - God in His Actuality, for God is real. God in His Ability, for God is Almighty. God in His wonderful Power to make and to do for us everything that is needed to be done - God in His Activity.

I. THE ACTUALITY OF GOD - "GOD IS"

The starting place is "God is". Knowledge is power. Human knowledge brings human power. Eternal knowledge brings eternal power. The knowledge of the Eternal God brings into our life a power that is greater than all the power that assails us. Greater is he that is within you than he that is in the world. You can bring all the powers of the world that are pressurising you and you can put before them the Actuality of God, for God outclasses them all.

God is greater than all of them. God is more powerful than all of them. They are not a match for God. God is sufficient and God gives sufficiency to His people.

John Knox was converted to Christ through the text - John 17: 3: "And this is life eternal, that they may know Thee the only true God, and Jesus Christ, Whom Thou hast sent." To be a partaker of the knowledge of God is the source of a power that can enable you to trample on all your worries, all your perplexities, all your adversities, all your enemies, and sing the song of divine deliverance.

He is the Ever-Present now: "God is". Get this into your heart, believer, get it into your soul, get it into your mind, make it your stay, make it your anchor, make it your creed, make it your faith - "God is". Those that come to God must believe that He is. "God is." God is Infinite. What does that mean? He is without bounds, He knows no limits, He fills all places and all things. We cannot imagine the extent of space, but there is nowhere in space where God is not the Infinite God. Go to the highest heavens, He is there. Make your bed in Hell, He is there. Go to the uttermost parts of the far flung universe, He is still there. God is Infinite. If the Infinite God be for us, who can be against us? God is eternal. From everlasting to everlasting Thou art God. God is eternal. He always was. He always will be. He knows neither past nor future; all is present with Him. We were singing about His Mystery this morning in that first hymn. When the pressures come upon you, and when it seems there are Everests that you cannot climb and oceans that you cannot swim and gulfs that you cannot bridge in 1995, get a grip with the hand of faith on the horn of this altar. God is eternal. The things of time are nothing, nothing, nothing to Him.

Secondly, God is not only infinite and eternal, God is immutable. He never changes: "I am the Lord, I change not, therefore ye sons of Jacob are not consumed." With Him is no variableness. There is not even the shadow of a turning. Let me make that truth practical to you. If God is immutable and He loved you yesterday, He is still loving you today. If you tasted something away back in your life's experience of the mighty love of God, He loves you still the same today. You might feel different. The toils, the labours, the strains might have told upon you, but they have not told in any way upon His love, His love is unchangeable, it never fades. Those that come unto God must believe that

He is, and without faith it is impossible to please God. When you are anchored in God and the storms hit your frail vessel, then you learn the truth that every storm that blows is just the slave of God, doing God's will.

I was reading in my private reading the other day, Psalm 148 and verse 8, and it says, "The stormy wind fulfilling His Word." When the stormy wind blows in 1995 do not think that some strange thing is happening unto you. Remember that the stormy wind fulfils His Word. "Jesus Christ the same", that is good. "Jesus Christ the same yesterday and today", that is better. "Jesus Christ the same forever", that is best. He is the unchangeable God.

II. THE ABILITY OF GOD - "GOD IS ABLE"

Let me turn from His Actuality - God is, and let me turn for a moment to His Ability - God is able. There is nothing that God cannot do except lie, for He is the God Who cannot lie. Now when I come to think about God's Ability I must first say, He is able, because He has all strength. The ability of a person to do a task rests in the strength that he has available to do that task. He may have a will to do it, but if he has not the strength he cannot do the job. But our God has all strength. How powerful is God! His Name is the Almighty. He can do everything He plans to do. He can perform everything He sets His mind to do. He can execute everything He declares He will do. God never fails. God cannot fail, and God will not fail. He has all strength. Everything He has purposed He will bring to fruition. He made choice of you in eternity. He could have passed you over. He did not need to choose you in Christ or me in Christ, but He did. Oh, the wonder of it! Oh, the wonder of it!

When He made choice of you in eternity He planned He would save you. He put the day on the calendar of His eternal purpose. He planned the circumstances of your conversion. He planned that that day you would come out of darkness into light, and you would be translated out of the power of sin and Satan unto God. Nobody believed that you would be converted. You did not believe you would be converted. But on that day God saved you. Why? Because God is able.

Then people said you would never keep it, as if we could keep anything! It is God who keeps the people He saves. You are a wonder to yourself and you are a wonder unto many that you are still on the road today. I want to tell you, you will be on the road because God is able. He is not only going to keep you through the temptations and the trials and troubles of life, but He is going to bring you safe to the Glory Land, and when you go through the pearly gates and stand on the golden streets and see the millions of angels and meet your loved ones and see Jesus, you know what you will shout? "God is able." Why? Because He has all strength. There is no limitation of His power. He never fainteth. He is never weary. He is the creator of the ends of the earth.

He is able also because He is all wisdom. You could have the power to do the job but if you had not the skill to do it, the power would be useless. God has not only the power but God has the wisdom. God's ways are perfect - perfect in planning, perfect in performing. God is able because He has all wisdom and nothing, nothing in Hell or on earth can alter one iota God's glorious, all-wise plan. His Covenant shall be fulfilled, every dot of every "i" and every stroke of every "t" will be fulfilled.

Thirdly, God is able because of His love. Love always finds a way. God's love has found a way to redeem His people, to cleanse them, to justify them, to sanctify them, and, glory to God, to glorify them. Love finds a way. Love scales unclimbable mountains. It spans unbridgeable gulfs. It sweeps immeasurable spheres. It searches unfathomable depths. It succeeds in unsolvable problems, and it sails uncrossable oceans - *the love of God:*

"O, 'twas love,
'twas wondrous love -
The love of God to me.

"It reaches into the bosom of God and it brought my Saviour down to die on Calvary. He is able because of His power. He is able because of His wisdom. He is able because of His love.

III. THE ACTIVITY OF GOD - "GOD IS ABLE TO MAKE ALL GRACE ABOUND TOWARD YOU; THAT YE, ALWAYS HAVING ALL SUFFICIENCY IN ALL THINGS, MAY ABOUND TO EVERY GOOD WORK."

I turn, finally, to the activity of God. Look at it with me: "God is able to make all grace abound toward you; that ye, always having all sufficiency in all things, may abound to every good work." Jesus Christ said: "My Father worketh hitherto; and I work." God is an active God. He is active on your behalf. God is working for you. All things work together for good to them that love God. You love God, do you not? Well, God is working for you, and He is working all things out after the counsel of His own will. Have you noted this text? There are three "Alls" in it. First of all it says, "All grace". Then it says, "All sufficiency". Then it says, "All things". If you have a good pair of glasses and you look at the *things* you will find it is in italics in your Authorised Version. It is not in the original. The text literally reads that we have all grace and all sufficiency in all, not just in all things but in all places, in all persons, in all situations, in all circumstances, in all plans. That last "All" takes in everything. Here we have an "All" that gives us the widest possible encouragement. You can be encouraged today. All is included in this promise. You see all those things that are worrying you, and sitting in the pew today you are thinking about what is going to happen tomorrow, are you not? You are thinking about something you have got to face on Wednesday, and you are thinking about something you have got to do on Friday, and you are sitting in God's House worrying. I want to tell you, this "All" takes them all in. It takes in Monday, Tuesday, Wednesday, Thursday, Friday, Saturday, all day Sunday, it takes in them all. This is for our encouragement today. All things are on the mind of God. Your Father cares for you. He cares for you far more than anybody else could care. He has an interest in you. You are not only His child, you are His heir. You are going to sit on the Throne with Him and He has a vested interest in His own elect people. "All grace" - There you have the fullest possible enrichment.

When I was sitting in my study today I was thinking about grace. I had an old Professor in school who believed in the old way of teaching, teaching by repetition. Today, of course, children don't even need to do tables, they have a little electric gadget and they just press the buttons and get the answer. I remember when my boys were doing their exams they took their little calculators with them. I said, "Why are you taking those?" "Oh, we are allowed to do that." This old Professor made me learn a definition of grace, and that must be some fifty years ago. It came back to me as clear this morning. "Grace is free, undeserved, unmerited favour of God, acting in full compliance with the exact unchangeable demands of His own nature through the Sacrifice of Christ on the Cross." Grace is more than love, it is love set absolutely free and made to be the triumphant victor against the righteous judgment of God against the sinner. That is what grace is. It is love without a boundary. It is love without a limit. It is love that cannot be defined.

"O, the deep, deep love of Jesus!
vast, unmeasured, boundless, free."

Put that against the troubles of 1995, and they will fade into insignificance. They are not worth a worry. God's love! There is something else, there is all-sufficiency.

Dean Alfred was a great Greek scholar. He wrote a fine work of four or five volumes on the Greek text of the New Testament. I pulled out a volume today to look at this word "All-sufficiency", and the great Greek scholar says: "It is an over-plus supply." That is what this word "sufficiency" means. It does not mean that you can do the job because you are sufficient to do it. It means that you can do the job, and if the job is a million times harder, you still can do it. You have an over-plus sufficiency. God does not send us out untrained, unskilled, unempowered to do His work, He gives us all sufficiency. You wonder how you will get through 1995. You have all-sufficiency in God. "Who is sufficient for these things?" The children of God are sufficient for these things. You know this, you are going to face three things in 1995. You are going to face the speeding-up of living. That is the great curse of our day, the speed of living. We are living in a rat race. People can't slow down, they are caught up with the increasing momentum of living that wears and tears our body, mind and soul.

Then the second thing is suspense. We are told by health specialists that the worst thing for the mind is suspense - the worst thing to strain the mind is suspense, anxiety, thinking of what might happen, thinking of what could happen, and even worrying about something that will never happen. Suspense! Then, strain. Paul said, (I started off with it, and I will end with it) he said he was pressed out of measure. Take the prefixes to that word "pressed". When you are pressed you become depressed. There are a lot of Christians depressed today. Some of you I am looking at look as if you are depressed, and it might be my sermon of course that is giving you that, and I can't blame you. Then there is such a thing as being suppressed, and many of you are suppressed. There is such a thing as being repressed, and such a thing as being oppressed.

All those things come when you are pressed out of measure, but God has an answer, He has an over-plus sufficiency for you, and you can meet the speed of the day, and you can meet the suspense of the day, and glory to God, you can meet the strain of the day, for you have all sufficiency. Could you get a better promise than that for 1995?

> *"I said to the man who stood at the gate of the year:*
> *Give me a light that I might tread the unknown,*
> *And he said, 'Go out and put your hand into the hand of God,*
> *That shall be better to you than a light and safer than any known way."*

Put your hand, child of God, in the nail-pierced hand of Christ. Christ is, Christ is able, Christ is able to make. If you are not a child of God become a child of God, today. Start the new year by repeating that simple prayer:

> *"I am coming, Lord, coming now to Thee,*
> *Wash me, cleanse me in the Blood*
> *That flowed on Calvary."*

And whosoever shall call on the Name of the Lord shall be saved. May it be so for Jesus' Sake.

AMEN AND AMEN!

7 Five
perpetualities

THIS BEING THE FIFTIETH anniversary of my ordination and my ministry on this road I was in prayer before God for a text - a special text for this year.

It has been my custom to have a Motto Text for each year of my ministry.

I was directed by the Spirit of God to the first chapter of the epistle of James and the verse five, and the first sentence of verse six: *"If any of you lack wisdom, let him ask of God, that giveth to all men liberally, and upbraideth not; and it shall be given him. But let him ask in faith, nothing wavering"*.

We have five perpetualities in this text.

Number one, you have the perpetual problem, *the lack of wisdom,* a problem that we all have, that dogs our footsteps from the cradle to the coffin, from childhood to old age. Lack of wisdom!

Number two, you have the perpetual prayer, *"Let him ask of God"*.

Number three, you have the perpetual Provider, *"God that giveth to all men liberally, and upbraideth not"*.

Number four, you have the perpetual promise, *"It shall be given him"*.

Number five, the vital perpetual precept, *"Let him ask in faith, nothing wavering"*.

As long as we travel in this old world of ours we will face trouble. Nineteen Hundred and Ninety-Six will be no different than any other year in which we have traversed this earth. In fact, in its unfolding it could bring to us more troubles than we have ever faced before. These troubles may not only be many in number but their character could be different to the trials we have experienced hitherto in life.

This Motto Text is specially suited for the trials and difficulties of Christian living and of Christian service. It is a seasonable Word. It is a Word for each day of the year. It is a Word for each hour and each moment of the year.

Let me stress. It is a practical Motto Text. It calls us not only to look at the Word but to obey it and experience its power in our hearts.

THE PERPETUAL PROBLEM

Let us look, first of all, at this perpetual problem, lack of wisdom, *"If any of you lack wisdom"*. Lack of wisdom is common to us all. It is the direct result of the fall of Adam and Eve who swallowed the bait which the devil held out to them. They thought they were going to be very wise indeed, and have the knowledge of good and evil. Instead they entered into the darkness of the fall and the blindness of sin, and as a result all of us are born lacking wisdom. Why?

Number one, **self-exaltedness.**

Self-exaltedness is the sin of pride, and pride brings blindness, and pride, of course, brings lack of wisdom. If we knew we were in a state of ignorance, if we knew that we were in a state of lack of knowledge, what would we do in the circumstances?

We would be instantly calling on God. It is because we do not confess this self-exaltedness, this pride that is in our hearts, we are not faithful in the matter of prayer and in the matter of calling upon the Lord.

Number two, hopelessness.

It is the great ploy of the devil to use hopelessness to depress and distress the people of God, and the despair begotten of hopelessness.

The devil suggests, "There is no hope for you. You might as well launch out in a career of sinning and pleasure. You might as well launch out in ungodly living, for God cannot forgive you." That is a lie from the pit but it results from lack of wisdom.

I have met Christians, and when you listen to them in their distress, reason has left them and they have lost all their wisdom simply because they have got into a state of hopelessness.

Number three, blindness.

Ignorance of Christian belief and ignorance of Christian behaviour produces in our lives this lack of wisdom. If we do not know God's Word then we lack wisdom. If we do not know how to apply God's Word to human situations and the hour of temptation, then we are lacking in wisdom.

That is why it is essential that the Word of God be expounded. It is however, not enough to expound God's Word. God's Word needs to be experienced. You might have head knowledge of the Book but if it is not a heartfelt experience then it is useless. Puffed up with head knowledge you will be an easy prey to the devil, to the world and to the flesh.

If you turn in your Bible to II Corinthians chapter four you will find there these words: *"In whom the god of this world hath blinded the minds of them which believe not."* Where there is no faith there will be blindness. That is the devil's work - to blind the minds of the people of God. Blindness is the fruit of unbelief. You remember it happened to Israel? We read in the epistle to the Romans that Israel was given over to unbelief, blinded by unbelief. Blindness is the fruit of sin, Jesus said, *"If thine eye be evil, thy whole body shall be full of darkness."*

Blindness comes as a judicial infliction by God upon His disobedient children. God withdraws His light from those that disobey Him. That is why you have backsliders that are as hard against Divine Truth as they can be. They are under judicial sentence - a sentence of blindness, *"For this cause many are weak and sickly among you, and many sleep. For if we would judge ourselves, we should not be judged."*

But if we do not judge ourselves, *"We shall be chastened of the Lord, that we should not be condemned with the world."*

"The natural man receiveth not the things of the Spirit."

When our heart becomes carnal we return to the natural pleasures that we enjoyed when we were ungodly and unsaved. We then begin to think more of this world than of the other world. We spend more time like ungodly people in trivia instead of seeking first the Kingdom of God and His righteousness. Lack of wisdom will characterise our lives. It is a perpetual problem among the people of God.

PERPETUAL PRAYER

There is a remedy, and the remedy is perpetual prayer. Look at that second part of the text, *"Let him ask of God"*. If you acknowledge today that you lack wisdom, if you acknowledge today, "Yes, there is pride in my heart. Yes, there is hopelessness at times in my soul. Yes, there is blindness in my whole spiritual life how am I going to remedy it?" It can be remedied in the way of perpetual prayer, "Let him ask of God". Let him ask!

In this incoming year you will face problems and there will be no way around those problems. You will face problems and there will be no way down under those problems to escape from them. Again there will be no way through those problems, and they will be so horrendous and terrible.

I say to you there is always a way up. I have been refreshing my mind recently in reading Mr Maxwell's books. Mr Maxwell was President of the Prairie Bible Institute in Canada. He wrote two great books - "Born Crucified" and "Crowded to Christ". Both books you should get and read, they have been reprinted. In his book "Crowded to Christ" he says that there was an officer in the American Flying Corps, and the officer wrote, "I was out over the ocean alone, and I saw in the distance coming rapidly towards me, a storm that was blacker than midnight. The black inky clouds seemed to be coming on with lightning rapidity. I knew I could not reach shore ahead of that storm. I looked down below thinking that perhaps if I went down as close to the sea I would escape the awful typhoon. Already however the sea was churning up and boiling in desperate fury. Knowing that the only hope I had was to rise above it, I turned my frail craft straight up towards the sky, a thousand feet; two thousand feet; two and a half thousand feet; three thousand feet; three thousand five hundred feet, and then the storm hit me. It was a hurricane, a cyclone and a typhoon all in one. The sky was blacker than any midnight. I never saw blackness like it, I could not see anything, I was enclosed in blackness. Rain came in torrents, snow began to fly, then the hail struck like bullets. I was at four thousand feet up and I knew that I must keep on climbing. When I had climbed to six thousand five hundred feet suddenly I was swept out into glorious sunlight, and a glory of a world that I had never been in before. Below me was the darkness of the storm, above me was the glorious sunshine of the clearest Heaven. I immediately began to repeat Scriptures to myself, and in the Heavens above the clouds I worshipped God."

In the storm of this incoming year, could I suggest to you that you need this perpetual prayer. Get hold of the joystick of prayer, direct your thoughts and your minds heavenward, upwards and upwards, and somewhere up there you will leave the darkness for the glorious light. You will leave the midnight for perfect midday. **"Ask of God"**. It is simple. Yet we are so filled with our own pride and our own wisdom that we will do anything rather than offer the perpetual prayer.

Could I say it does not say "Ask the priest". You will notice that. It does not say "Ask the preacher", nor does it say "Ask the learned men". No, it says, "Ask of God".

In one of Mr Spurgeon's sermons he says "We need to remember the absolute necessity of the work of the Holy Spirit in our lives." He said he often prayed the following prayer, *"O, Father, Thou hast been pleased to reveal to us the Holy Spirit Who is to lighten our darkness and remove our ignorance. O, let that Spirit of Thine dwell in me. I am willing to be taught of Thy Spirit through Thy Word or through Thy ministers, but I come first to Thee because I know that Thy Word and Thy ministers, apart from Thyself, cannot teach me anything. O Lord, teach Thou me, give me Thy Holy Spirit."*

I would suggest that that prayer should be upon all our lips continually. Ask God to cleanse away the pride, to take away the spirit of hopelessness, to take away the blindness; to increase your faith, and acknowledge your total and absolute dependence upon God Almighty alone.

THE PERPETUAL PROVIDER

Let us turn to the third point. *The Perpetual Provider. "God that giveth to all men liberally, and upbraideth not."*

Notice three things- *"God that giveth to all men."*
First, there is no reservation.

God does not reserve His giving to some special order of Christians. God does not reserve His giving to Christians older and stronger in the faith than the young children just born into the Kingdom of God. There is absolutely no reservation here. Notice what the text has to say, *"That giveth to all men"*. Notice how it starts, *"If any man"*. Any man! There is no reservation here. Thank God the circle of this text includes me! Thank God the circle of this text includes anyone who wants to stand in its centre and claim it as his divine privilege and right as a child of God, *"If any man"*. God giveth to all men.

Your needs may be like a mighty leviathan. Well, here is a sea of promise where that mighty leviathan can swim forever. There is no boundary to it. It has no brim. It has no shore and it has no bottom.

Your needs may seem elephant-like in size, but here is an ark where that elephant can find a sanctuary and be safe.

Your needs may be so gigantic that you wonder how God can meet them. Here is a promise that is fitted to every need that you ever had, and to every need you now have and to every need you ever will have. This is the promise of God.

Notice secondly, *"He giveth to all men liberally"*. There is no limitation.

There is no reservation. God is not a stingy giver. There are some of God's people and they are stingy givers. I remember William Weir saying to me, "When I first went to India, Ian, it was the custom that the Christians all went down to the docks, and as the boat pulled out to go to Liverpool to take us to the ocean liner that would take us to our mission field, they all sang 'God be with you 'till we meet again'. Hundred of people were there." And Willie said to me, "I'm glad God was with me, the vast majority of those people never sent me a sixpence." They were stingy, but God is not stingy. God gives liberally. He gives most liberally.

Let me tell you, there is something more in this text. No reservation, no limitation, but there is something more, "He upbraideth not". There is no condemnation.

In one of his books C H Spurgeon tells the story of a preacher who got into debt and he owed the sum of something like £30.00, which was a colossal amount of money in those days.

He wrote to a very wealthy preacher in London, and he told him of his need. The wealthy preacher came down to his home and read this man a stern lesson of the curse of debt and why we should not get into debt. After he preached to him for ten minutes he took out a five pound note and he put it into his hand. Then he preached another sermon to him, and then he put another five pound note into his hand. Then he preached another sermon to him, and the sermons got more fiery, more cruel, and more cutting. The debtor was standing sobbing and he put another fiver into his hand until he had given him the thirty pounds. Finally he said, "Good-day to you, never get into debt again."

God does not deal with His people like that. It is the hand of love with which God gives. He does not scold you. He does not say, "You are an old reprobate, Paisley. You should never have got into the trouble you have got yourself into. You have done despite to my Spirit. You do not deserve my pardon. I will forgive you, Paisley, but I will never forget it."

Goes does not treat us like that. "God giveth to all men liberally, and upbraideth not". No condemnation! No limitation! No reservation! No condemnation! This is the great God whom we have to trust in Nineteen Ninety-Six. What a God He is! God's heart is made of tenderness, His bowels melt with love. Do not be afraid to go to the Covenant God of Israel.

THE PERPETUAL PROMISE

Notice the perpetual promise, *"and it shall be given him"*.

I wondered why this needed to be added. If that verse had just read *"If any of you lack wisdom, let him ask of God, that giveth to all men liberally and upbraideth not ..."* that would have been good enough, would it not? No, that would not be good enough, because great faith could take the inference from the text, but little faith must have it set out in the plainest possible language.

All through the Bible God's promises, Hallelujah, are in the simplest possible language. You can't dispute them.

How can you dispute the text, *"God so loved the world, that He gave His only begotten Son, that whosoever believeth in Him should not perish, but have everlasting life."* "Whosoever". John Bunyan said, when he was under conviction of sin, "Oh, if it had only said if John Bunyan believes in Him he will not perish." Then he thought, well, there are other John Bunyans in the world, how would I know this John Bunyan was me?

The Holy Ghost said, "That is why I wrote it there, 'Whosoever'". It is a simple word, it is a word of clarity and clearness. Here is a simple word **"it shall be given him"**.

Is God a liar? No, He is the God Who cannot lie. This is the unchallengable, impregnable, inerrant, infallible Word of the Living God. Can you not walk out into the troubles of this year with this bright promise shining in your soul? "It shall be given him."

Do you want to see your family saved, mother? It shall be given you. Do you want to see your loved ones in Christ? It shall be given you. Do you want to see a revival of religion? It shall be given you. Do you want to see sick ones healed? It shall be given you. Do you want to see wounds cleansed? It shall be given you. Do you want to see darkness dispelled? It shall be given you. Do you want the rough places to be made smooth? It shall be given you. Do you want the crooked places to be made straight? It shall be given you.

There is not a problem nor a difficulty which my God cannot solve.

This is what the Book is saying to us. Trust God. Do not trust yourself. Do not trust fellow Christians. Trust God. He that trusteth God will never be ashamed.

Believer, here is a door. It never opens to push you out from grace. It always opens to shut you unto grace. God's doors do not close to push you out, they close to shut you in. All through the Bible we read of doors that God used to shut men into His goodness, to shut men into His grace, to shut men into His love, and to shut men into His deliverance. The perpetual promise, *"It shall be given him."*

THE PERPETUAL PRECEPT

The perpetual precept *"Let him ask in faith, nothing wavering."*

Those that come to God must believe that He is. I do not have difficulty with that, I believe that God is. I only have to look at the heavens. They declare the Glory of God and the firmament sheweth His handiwork. The workmanship of creation is beyond the workmanship of men. There must be a Mind so Wise, a Power so Great and a Person so Majestic, that He could call this whole world into orbit and keep the stars in place, and the earth revolving, and all the heavens in order. It was so simple for Him to do so. The words describing the starry heavens and creation are in a very short little sentence in Genesis chapter one, *"He made the stars also"* The stars also!

Man thinks he has accomplished something when he puts a little space-ship out into orbit, and he glories in what he has done. What spaceships of magnitude God created on that great creation day. He lifted them in His hand and threw them out into the starry expanse of heaven. They are all revolving in the orbit which He planned for them, and will go on in that orbit until the day He calls them to cease and perish forever.

I do not have difficulty with that, but I confess I have difficulty with the second part. We must believe that he is the Rewarder of those that diligently seek Him.

If we really believe that, we would diligently seek Him. If there is one thing which does not characterise the prayers of this church, and the prayers of this people and the prayers of this preacher, it is diligently seeking God.

Diligence means that you address this matter with the totality of your being. You let nothing stop you. You let nothing keep you back. You cut every tie. You break every chain. You give yourself to this work. It is a matter of life and death to your soul.

When we get life-or-death praying in this House, God will send revival.

In the old Church people objected to the vocabulary of men praying in the prayer meetings.

They said: "Those men, Mr Paisley, are ordering God about, their language should not be tolerated."

I said, "Just a minute, the Bible says, 'Ye are the Lord's remembrancers. The Kingdom of Heaven suffereth violence, and the violent take it by force.'"

A prominent pressman who attended a service in the early days of this building wrote about it like this, "Paisley stood in his pulpit and he pleaded with

God, and he pleaded with such fervour and fire that I said, 'O God, give him what he wants and let him shut up.'" Give him what he wants!

We should pray prayers which beseech God's Throne until God says, "I will reward you."

There is a story in the Scripture about that. The Lord told it.

A woman came to an unjust judge, and she said continually, "I want justice for myself." At long last the unjust judge said, "I am not going to give her justice because she deserves it, or because she qualifies for it. She is, however, wearying me. I am getting sick of her at my door and on my doorstep."

The Lord said, "If the unjust judge avenged the widow, how much more shall your Heavenly Father give you what you want." You do not need to push hard on God's door until He opens it!

AMEN AND AMEN

8 The right hand
of Christ

TURN IN YOUR BIBLE to the first chapter of the Book of the Revelation, and look with me at the verse 16: *"And He* (that is our Lord Jesus Christ) *had in His right hand seven stars: and out of His mouth went a sharp two-edged sword: and His countenance was as the sun shineth in his strength".*

For many years when my revered father was alive he used to give me a motto text for each year, and I used to preach upon that text which he faithfully sent to me. Since his decease I have had to do my own digging for my motto text, but I am amazed that as each year unfolds, the application of that text becomes more and more telling and more and more appropriate. What better text could we have had for last year: "If any man lack wisdom, let him ask of God". If ever there was a year that we needed wisdom it was 1996, and if ever there was a year that we received divine wisdom it was 1996.

My attention for this year has been drawn to this great text in the vision of John exiled for the Word of God and the testimony of Jesus Christ. Alone, isolated, imprisoned with an embargo upon his ministry, and separation from the church in which he was the preacher, the church at Ephesus. When he got up on the Lord's Day he did not get up in misery, like some people do on the Lord's Day, he got up in the Spirit on the Lord's Day, and he had the vision, and what a vision, of the wonderful Son of Man!

You will notice three things about Christ in this text. You have His hand. You have His mouth, and you have His face. But notice the emphasis is upon the grasp of Christ's hand. What does it say? "He had in His right hand seven stars".

I want to speak, first of all, upon the Grasp of His hand. Then secondly, we have the emphasis upon His mouth, the Gospel of His mouth: "A sharp two-edged sword went out of His mouth". The Gospel of Christ's mouth. Then, last of all, we are confronted with the face of Jesus, the Glory of Christ's face: "His countenance was as the sun shineth in his strength".

THE GRASP OF CHRIST'S HAND

Let us look, first of all, at the grasp of Christ's hand: "He had in His right hand seven stars". If you come down to verse 20 you will find who the stars were: "The mystery of the seven stars which thou sawest in my right hand. The seven stars are the angels of the seven churches".

When I was a boy I often wondered who the angel of the church was. I knew there were many women who claimed to be angels, but when you got to know them you were assured that they were fallen ones. I discovered, when I was older, that this word translated "angel" in our Authorised Version, "angelos" in the Greek text, is the word "messenger" or "minister", and, as there were seven churches, so there was one minister for each church. This blows to smithereens the church policy of Plymouth Brethrenism which tells us there is no such thing as a minister of the church. It was Mr Spurgeon who said: "Is it not strange when the Lord wrote to the churches in the New Testament he did not write to the Oversight, he wrote to the minister who was responsible to bring God's message to the people". The minister of the church! It is interesting to notice that the emphasis is put upon the awful responsibility; the terrifying responsibility that the minister has as the minister of the church. But for the encouragement of the minister we discover the grasp of Christ's hand. He holds the minister in His right hand. The hand of Christ!

If you look with me at verse 13 you will find that we have a title of Christ there. "And in the midst of the seven candlesticks one like unto the Son of Man". That title, Son of Man, lays particular emphasis on the Humanity of our

Lord Jesus Christ. We read in Hebrews chapter 4 and verse 15: "for we have not an high priest which cannot be touched with the feeling of our infirmities; but was in all points tempted like as we are, yet without sin". So the emphasis is upon Christ's Humanity, that is, He knows by experience. He cares because He has been in the same dark valley. He can set Himself alongside us. The Holy Spirit is called the Comforter, the One called alongside to help. But remember Jesus said, "I will send you another Comforter," and Jesus Christ is alongside us to help.

You will notice also three other titles of Christ in the chapter. Verse 5, He is "the faithful witness", He is "the first begotten of the dead", and "the Prince of the kings of the earth".

The Shorter Catechism tells us that Christ exercises three Offices on the part of His people. He is a Prophet, He is a Priest and He is a King. Here we have these three offices. He is a faithful witness, that is the Prophetic Office. He is the first begotten of the dead, that is the Priestly Office, and He is the Prince of the kings of the earth, that is the Kingly Office.

Who is it that grasps in His hand the minister of the church? It is none other than the Son of Man, with all His tenderness, with all His sympathy, with all His fellow-feeling, with all His experience of our griefs. The Man of Sorrows and acquainted, not ignorant of, but acquainted with our griefs, the Great Prophet, the Great Priest, and the Great King of the church.

THE RIGHT HAND OF CHRIST

Notice carefully what hand it is. It is the right hand. The hand of God relates to nine things in the Bible. It relates to His Eternal purpose and executive power. It relates to His Providential bounty and goodness. It relates to His mighty power to preserve and to defend. It relates to His frowns and His corrections. It relates to His Sovereign disposals. It relates to His help. It relates to His favour. It relates to His Spirit, and it relates to His Providence. All those things are mentioned in relation to Christ's hand in the Bible. But the right hand puts its emphasis upon the power and strength and All-mightiness of God. "Thy right hand, O Lord, is become glorious in power. Thy right hand, O God, hath dashed in pieces the enemy" Exodus 15:6. So the emphasis here is upon the strength of the Lord's hand.

I am glad, today, that as I enter this fifty-first year of my ministry, and as I look out upon a world that is filled with darkness, and gloom, and turmoil, and blasphemy and apostasy that I am in the right hand of the Almighty God.

THE NAIL-PIERCED HAND - THE WOUNDED HAND

Notice, secondly, this is the nail-pierced hand, it is the wounded hand.

I was thinking last night as I was preparing this message, that the minister is pressed continually to the wounds of the Son of God. In His hands he is pressed to the scars, and it is only as the shadow of Calvary rests upon us, it is only as the wounds of Jesus and the scars of Jesus are pressed into our soul by the clasp of Christ that we can be the servant of God as we ought to be. This is not a once and for all experience, this is a constant, continuous and never-ending experience, for the preacher must never leave the Cross.

Why do we have apostasy in our land today? Because preachers have left the Cross. Why do we have backsliding in the church? Because Christians have left the Cross. Why do we see so much evil on earth? Because the Cross is not preached.

"For the preaching of the Cross is to them that perish foolishness, but unto us who are saved it is the power of God". The hymnwriter wrote the words,

Near the Cross, a trembling soul,
Love and mercy found me.
There the Bright and Morning Star
Shed its beams around me.

Near the Cross I'll watch and wait,
Hoping, trusting ever.
'Till I reach the golden strand,
Just beyond the river.

In the Cross, In the Cross,
Be my glory ever
'Till my ransomed soul shall find
Rest beyond the river.

THE GRASPING HAND OF THE SAVIOUR

It is not only the right hand of the Saviour, and the nail-pierced hand - the wounded hand of the Saviour, but it is the grasping hand, held by the power of that hand. Turn in your Bible to John's Gospel chapter 10 and there is a word that we would do well to mark, a word of encouragement to us all. John's Gospel at the chapter 10 tells us in verse 28, "My sheep hear my voice, and I know them, and they follow me. And I give unto them eternal life; and they shall never perish, neither shall any man pluck them out of my hand." Once grasped by the hand of Jesus we are grasped with an Eternal Unbreakable grasp - the grasp of the Son of God.

A LIFE-GIVING HAND

Notice, as you come back to the first chapter of Revelation you will find that this is a life-giving hand. When the Lord spoke to John something happened. When he saw His right hand, when he saw His mouth, when he saw His countenance, "And when I saw Him (verse 17) I fell at His feet as dead. And He laid (the same hand) his right hand upon me, saying unto me, Fear not; I am the first and the last: I am He that liveth, and was dead; And, behold, I am alive for evermore". The Life-giving hand! In the hand of Christ the Life of the Saviour is imparted to the one who is grasped near the wounds of Jesus.

THE SOVEREIGN HAND OF CHRIST

Lastly, notice please, it is a Sovereign hand. He says, "I have the keys of Hell and of Death".

Do you think that your Saviour will ever use those keys to lock you into Hell, or lock you into Eternal death - the second death? The answer is, never! He is the only One who could incarcerate us there but He will never do that. He holds those keys so that no power in Heaven, no power on earth, no power under the earth, no power in Hell will ever lock a child of God into the imprisonment of everlasting darkness and eternal punishment. He is the Custodian. He is the Keeper of the keys. The Pope says he has the power of the keys, and on ceremonial occasions he carries keys that do not fit any lock, that open no doors, and, in fact, are powerless, but thank God, Christ has the power of the keys. In His right hand they are, and in His right hand they ever will be.

Who are in His hands? It is very noticeable, is it not, that these ministers of Christ are described as stars. You never see the stars in the daytime. When the sun comes up the stars cannot be seen. There must be night before you can see the stars, and the darker the night the brighter is the light of those stars.

In 1997 there will be a year of intense darkness, darkness will increase over this earth of ours and gross darkness the people. I have been asking God that He will help me to shine more brightly in the darkness. I have been asking God to help me to shine more and more brightly amidst the darkness. Oh, my God, let me shine for Jesus in 1997! On the right hand of the Majesty on High there sits the right handed Christ, and that right handed Christ holds the stars amidst the darkness. May God help us to shine as lights among men!

These stars were made by Christ, He made them. Once they were in darkness, but now they are light in the Lord. The Bible says that we are to be harmless, the sons of God without rebuke in the midst of a crooked and perverse nation, among whom ye shine as lights in the world. If there ever was a perverse and crooked nation it is our own nation today. I see now that in the gambling machines they have decided by Government Order to put up the winnings, so as to encourage people to gamble more, and we are going to enter this millennium on the money of gambling.

I said from this pulpit that the Government, before it ended, would turn this nation into a nation of gamblers. The Prime Minister has the audacity to claim that his Government produces three millionaires a week. How many paupers does his Government produce on the back of the gambling demon? That is the question that needs to be asked.

We are to shine as lights amidst this crooked generation.

I was interviewed by an atheist lady for a programme on the Ten Commandments, which will be played each Monday morning at 8.45 am. We had a very good exchange on that particular interview. It will be broadcast later on in the month, but she was maintaining there was no God, therefore people did not need to obey God's commandments. I asked her what was the difference between her and an animal if there was no God. I said, "The difference is that you have got a conscience. Have you a conscience?" She said, "I have," and she said, "I must admit that that is the dividing line between a beast and man. A beast has no conscience, the man has." I said, "What is the conscience? It is the mechanism that God has put into us all which either accuses us or excuses us in our behaviour. Now, could you tell me why every one that breaks the Commandments feels the accusation of conscience?" I said, "There was an atheist preaching atheism in the House of Commons the other day, and I asked him would he like me to go over and take his wallet, because the Ten Commandments did not matter, 'Thou shalt not steal' did not matter, so I would be quite entitled, if he went on preaching that philosophy, to go over and steal his money." He had no answer. Of course it is only a fool that says in his heart "There is no God".

WHY ARE GOD'S MINISTERS THERE?

Why are they there? They are there because God placed them there. All the education in the world, all the natural talents ever possessed, all the acquired prowess of oratory, all the gains that result from long experience, can never make a Christian minister. Only God can make a star for the hand of Christ. Only God can do it. If God does not make a man a minister then he is an imposter as he stands before his people. They are there because God made choice of them. They are there because God made them. They are there because God upholds them. Ministers are in the front line. The sharpest of the Devil's arrows will be shot at them. The vilest of the Devil's slanders will be spread about them. The fiercest of temptations will be laid before them. The darkest and bloodiest of conflicts will be planned for them. Every kind of evil will pursue them like wild dogs. The minister has to pray every day one prayer - the prayer of David, "Hold Thou me up and I shall be safe". Ah, but does not the Lord hold the star - the minister - up in His hand?

Could I say, fifthly, they are in His hand because He holds them forth. You see, if you have a light and you are going on a dark path, you hold that light as far before you as you can, so that its light will light up as far as possible the road you have got to travel. That is what God does with His ministers, they are His stars and He holds them far out into the darkness so that the light may reach the recesses where men are blinded by the god of this world, lest the light of the glorious Gospel of Christ should shine into their hearts.

Lastly, could I say the ministers are in His hand because He gives them the greatest honour that He can bestow.

Thomas Goodwin, the great Puritan writer said, "God has only one Son, and He made Him a Minister". There is no higher honour that could be given to any son of man than to be a minister of Jesus Christ. We do not need the honours and the praises of fallen men, I do not want to be called a thoughtful man, or a learned man, or a clever man or a statesman. Those labels are only for the scavengers of this apostate age. I just want to be known as a man who does the will of God and who preaches the Word of God. Oh, to shine for Christ! Oh, to shine for nothing but Christ! Oh, to shine with nothing but Christ's Light! Oh, to shine for Christ and for Christ alone and forever!

I trust that you will pray for me this year, that I may be a morning star in Christ's hand in 1997, heralding the breaking of the morning of a great revival, when God will revive His church and bless His people.

PART TWO

The sixteenth verse of the first chapter of Revelation, "And He had in His right hand seven stars." The **Grasp of the Saviour's Hand**. "And out of His mouth went a sharp two-edged sword" - the **Gospel of the Saviour's Mouth**. "And his countenance was as the sun shineth in His strength" - **the Glory of the Saviour's Face.**

THE GOSPEL OF HIS MOUTH

I want to look, first of all, at the Gospel of His Mouth. Having considered in the first message the wonder of the Grasp of His Hand.

Notice, please, and keep in mind ever that the invincible power of the Gospel is from Christ Himself. The seven stars are not mentioned in regard to the Saviour's mouth. They are linked with the Saviour's grasp, because the power of the Gospel has nothing whatsoever to do with the preacher, he has the glory in an earthen vessel, that the excellency of the power may be of God, and not of us.

The preacher is impotent, the Saviour is Omnipotent. He has the power. The power which vanquishes Satan, overcomes sin, subdues self, dispels darkness, slays apostasy, destroys the Antichrist and devastates iniquity, comes from the mouth of the Saviour Himself, not from the mouth of the preacher.

We shine as preachers, or ought to shine, as stars. What does a star do? It just reflects the shining of the sun.

The sharp two-edged sword comes from the mouth of Christ and Christ alone. If Christ be not present the Gospel is powerless. If Christ is not present, the Gospel does not save, for it is only in the hand of Christ that the sharp two-edged sword of power can be wielded with saving strength. Without Him we can do nothing. Some preachers claim that they are God's right-hand men. They are no such thing. God does not have any right-hand men, but Christ holds the true preacher in His right hand. God depends not upon man, for the flesh profiteth nothing. We are not the real warriors in this battle. We only follow the Captain of our salvation. He already devastates the foe and destroys the serried ranks of His enemies. We follow, like David's mighty men, just to take the prey.

Notice also, the Gospel in Christ's mouth is as the **power of a sword**. That sword is the Word of God. Turn in your Bible over to that great epistle of Hebrews, and in that great epistle in verse 12 of chapter 4 we read this: *"For the Word of God is quick, and powerful, and sharper than any two-edged sword, piercing even to the dividing asunder of soul and spirit, and of the joints and marrow, and is a discerner of the thoughts and intents of the heart. Neither is there any creature that is not made manifest in His sight: but all things are naked and open unto the eyes of Him with whom we have to do."*

THE DISCERNING SWORD

Three things are taught here concerning the sword. First of all, it is a **discerning sword**. It discerns the thoughts and intents of the heart. I could preach with all my might and with all my power, and exercise all given talents that God has bestowed on me, but I could not with that discern the thoughts and intents of the heart. Only this weapon, only this sword can lay naked and open the whole heart before God. Your heart, when God applies His Word, is laid open before God.

I was reading this week the history of that great seminary in America, it was well known, before new evangelism took it over, for its fundamentalism and evangelism, Princeton Seminary. The first Professor of that Seminary was a great revival preacher, Archibald Alexander. In the revivals men sat in the pew and bent over and wept. Do you know what they said? They cried out, "How does the preacher know what is in my sinful heart?" The preacher did not know what was in their sinful heart, but the Word of God laid their heart naked and open before God.

I pray God that very soon in this Province we shall see this naked two-edged sword laying open men's hearts and exposing the intents of their soul so they will cry out, "How does the preacher know the dark villainy and satanic impurity of my soul?" A discerner of the thoughts and intents of the heart. May God apply the sword to our hearts today!

The prayerlessness of God's people is a crying shame. It sends a reek of abomination to Heaven and must cry out against God's people. The neglect of the Holy Word of God, how the Book of God is neglected today among the saints of God! The trivialities, the excuses that are sent by God's people to keep them from activity for Christ. Oh, my friend, it is time the sword laid naked the thoughts and intents of the heart.

THE DIVIDING SWORD

This sword is not only a discerning sword, it is a **dividing sword**. It pierces even to the dividing asunder. Notice what it divides asunder, the soul and the spirit. I have never in any volume of theology found any satisfying definition explaining the difference between soul and spirit. There are two views in theology. There is a view that man is dual and he just has a spiritual part and a physical part, and you can call the spiritual part his soul, or his spirit if you care. It is one and the same thing, and he has a physical part. There is another view which I believe is the Scriptural view, that man is tripartite. He has a body, he has a soul and he has a spirit.

I remember asking my Dad once to explain to me the difference between soul and spirit, and he said, "The only way, son, you will learn the difference is to get the word of God and it will divide the soul and the spirit." The Supreme Divider is the sword. It not only divides the evil and the good, but it divides the soul from the spirit.

What a sword this must be when it divides asunder the very things that are so closely linked that men cannot discern or define their difference.

DEATH-DEALING SWORD

The third thing I want you to notice, it is not only a discerning sword, it is not only a dividing sword, but it is a **death-dealing sword**.

Immediately the Lord Jesus Christ spoke to John, what happened to him? "I fell at His feet as dead." It is a death-dealing sword. Self-righteousness, carnal trust, cannot stand before this sword. One Word from Christ to a man's soul will do more in a second of time than tens of thousands of the most eloquent sentences from a gospel preacher. One Word. That is why we need to pray "Oh Christ speak, loose the sword, let it discern, let it divide, let it deal death to that which is not of Thee."

Please notice there is something about this sword that is emphasised. It is a **sharp** sword.

How sharp is that sword! That sword which is of the Lord's making, and bears a steel which has been tempered in the fires of eternity, is shaped and sharpened by the hand of God Himself.

Notice it is all edge, it is a sharp two-edged sword, there is no back to it.

It is interesting to note that when the Gospel of Christ is preached and Christ uses that sword, then those who need those two edges upon their inner being will feel the strength and sharpness of both. At times I have preached for the comforting of the saints, but as I preached God was slaughtering a sinner in the meeting, and using His sword to flay that sinner, and at the end of the meeting while the saints were comforted that sinner was struck with conviction which led to Christ. Why? Because the sword of Christ was present.

STICK TO THE OLD SWORD

There are those who tell us today that the days of preaching are past, that the church must adapt itself to new methodology in order to attract the ears of those who will not attend to truth. The fact is that the churches who adopt worldly methods become more and more emptied, the prayer pews are forsaken and the Gospel pulpit is forgotten, and the Bible is neglected, and the church corrupts and perishes.

We need to remember that our future as a church is to stick to the old sword. It is like Goliath's blade, and what did David say to the high priest when he said, "I have only one sword here, it is the sword of Goliath," and David said, "There is none like it, give it me."

You remember the first time David used that sword he used it to cut off the head of that great adversary of the people of God. "There is none like it, give it me."

In good report or in evil report, in days when the tide goes out and in days when the tide comes in, in days of declension and dearth, in days of revival and fruitbearing, there is only one method which saves men, and that is this mighty sword, not exercised by man but blessed by Christ Himself.

Oh, Mighty Saviour, open Thy mouth today! Let that sharp two-edged sword deal its blows on everything within my heart that is contrary to Thy will! Let it lay naked my heart before Thee, so that I might prepare my way in consecration to be totally and absolutely in Thy hand for service! May that be the prayer of us all, Oh, let us hear the Sword once more striking home divine truth to the hearts of both the saints and the sinners.

THE GLORY OF HIS FACE

Let me turn to the last part of my text, the **Glory of His face**.

The greatest prayer ever prayed by any man in the Scriptures was the prayer of Moses. What was that prayer? "Shew me thy Glory", and God shewed Moses His Glory and Moses was never the same. After that no one could look upon Moses. He had to veil his face. The only time Moses was ever seen after that with unveiled face was when he entered the Tabernacle and talked with God face to face. At all other times the children of Israel never again saw the face of Moses. Why? Because his face was lit up with the Glory of Christ.

Turn with me in the New Testament to II Corinthians 3:17, a text that is much repeated and very often completely misquoted. *"Now the Lord is that Spirit: and where the Spirit of the Lord is, there is liberty."* What does that mean? People would say that is fluency in prayer, that is fluency in preaching, that is fluency in praising. Well I want to tell you it is nothing of the sort, it has nothing to do with fluency. Look at the context of the text, look at verse 16, *"Nevertheless when it shall turn to the Lord, the veil shall be taken away"* It is liberty for the veil to be removed. What veil? The veil that kept the glory from being seen.

Look at verse 18: *"But we all, with open face beholding as in a glass the glory of the Lord, are changed into the same image from glory to glory, even as by the Spirit of God."*

You and I in this Gospel Age can have, every day, the experience of Moses. You, because this is the Gospel day when the full blessing of Christ is poured out without measure, can be changed from glory to glory, beholding the face of our Lord Jesus.   ·

I was struck, when I read that great chapter in Revelation, that the highest thing in heaven is that they see the Saviour's face. That is the highest thing, that is what brings the glory and ecstasy of Heaven home to the hearts of all who are there. We can however see the face of Jesus upon this earth.

When I was a lad in Sunday School they used the *Redemption Hymn Book*, and number 438 in that Hymn Book was often sung:

I've seen the face of Jesus,
He smiled in love on me.
I: filled my heart with rapture,
My soul with ecstasy.
The scars of deepest anguish
Were lost in glory bright.
I've seen the face of Jesus
It was a wondrous sight.

And since I've seen His Beauty,
All else I count but loss.
The World, its fame and pleasure
Is now to me but dross.
His light dispels my darkness,
His smile was, oh, so sweet.
I've seen the face of Jesus
I can but kiss His feet.

O glorious face of beauty!
Oh, gentle touch of care
If here it is so blessed
What will it be up there?

Please note what it says in my text: *"His countenance was as the sun shineth in its strength."* When the sun comes out the stars all disappear. There is a mention of the stars in the first part of my text, you have starlight, but my text ends with sunlight, and where sunlight is no stars are seen. When God obliterates the preacher, and when the Lord Jesus Christ is seen in all His Majestic Glory, and when the Sun of Righteousness arises upon our souls with healing in His wings it is like the sun in its brilliance, in its meridian, in the fullness of its strength.

Sometimes in church history God has given a sun-blink of Jesus to His church. There was a man who wrote the history of revivals, a man by the name of Fleming, and he said, "The periods that I am going to talk about are when we had sun-blinks from Jesus, and the church saw her Lord."

When the church saw her Lord, her Lord was robed in inconceivable and inexpressible glory. Oh, the eternal splendour of our Lord Jesus. He is the centre of heaven. What is the centre of heaven? The Throne! Who is at the centre of the heavenly Throne? The Lamb in the midst of the Throne. No man can look upon the sun when it shineth in its strength and keep his eyesight. On the Damascus Road Saul the persecutor got a glimpse of the sun, and he was blind for three days and three nights. He said it was above the brightness of the sun. In the blinding brilliance of that shining, angels have to veil their faces. The angels do not have eyes that can take the glory of the Saviour so they use their wings to veil their faces and they utter only one cry in His presence, "Holy, Holy, Holy, Lord God Almighty". But "Blessed are the pure in heart for they shall see God."

THE PURE IN HEART

Brethren and sisters in Christ, let me tell you, upon this earth you can see God if you are pure in heart. It is because impurities control us, it is because unjudged sins rule us, it is because we sit so near to the world and so far away from walking in the full light of heaven that we do not see Him, but thank God we can see Him.

I was thinking this week of Psalm 139. Just turn to it, and with this I will close. In that Psalm we have some verses we need to ponder carefully. Verses 14 and 15, *"I will praise Thee; for I am fearfully and wonderfully made: marvellous are Thy works; and that my soul knoweth right well. My substance was not hid from Thee, when I was made in secret, and curiously wrought in the lowest parts of the earth. Their eyes did see my substance, yet being unperfect; and in Thy Book all my members were written, which in continuance were fashioned, when as yet there was none of them."* I can say that of my birth, so could the Lord Jesus. Who fashioned the Body of Christ?

The Bible tells us "The Father prepared a body for His Son." I want you to think about that just for a moment - the preparing of Christ's Body. Who was it that decided what the colour of His eyes would be? Who was it that pencilled the particular line of every part of His Body? It was the Father. You know why? Because the Son is the express image of the Father, and the Father was portraying Himself in the Precious Body of Christ. In the Book that was written all His members were written, which in continuance were fashioned, when as yet there was none of them.

THE FACE OF JESUS

When the Father shaped the face of Jesus and looked upon it He knew that it was a face for the spitting. He knew it was the face for the beating. He knew it was the face for the battering and He knew it was the face for the bleeding.

The Father made that face that was going to be marred more than any man, and the form of it more than the sons of men. What a face is the face of Christ! Yes, the hymn that I quoted is absolutely right.

"The scars of deepest anguish
Were lost in Glory bright.
I've seen the face of Jesus,
It is a lovely sight.

O, Glorious face of beauty,
O, gentle touch of love!
If here it is so blessed
What will it be above?"

Please God, every man and woman and boy and girl in this house today will see the face of Jesus! You will never be the same again if you see His face.

AMEN AND AMEN!

9 The centrality
of Christ

TURN TO THE OLD TESTAMENT, to the prophecy of Joel chapter 2:21-32 *"Fear not, O land; be glad and rejoice; for the Lord will do great things. Be not afraid, ye beasts of the field: for the pastures of the wilderness do spring, for the tree beareth her fruit, the fig tree and the vine do yield their strength Be glad then, ye children of Zion, and rejoice in the Lord your God: for he hath given you the former rain moderately, and he will cause to come down for you the rain, the former rain, and the latter rain in the first month. And the floors shall be full of wheat, and the fats shall overflow with wine and oil. And I will restore to you the years that the locust hath eaten, the cankerworm, and the caterpillar, and the palmerworm, my great army which I sent among you. And ye shall eat in plenty and be satisfied, and praise the name of the Lord your God, that hath dealt wondrously with you: and my people shall never be ashamed. And ye shall know that I am in the midst of Israel, and that I am the Lord your God, and none else: and my people shall never be ashamed. And it shall come to pass afterward, that I will pour out my spirit upon all flesh; and your sons and your daughters shall prophesy, your old men shall dream dreams, your young men shall see visions: And also upon the servants and upon the handmaids in those days will I pour out my spirit. And I will shew wonders in the heavens and in the earth, blood, and fire,* *and pillars of smoke. The sun shall be turned into darkness, and the moon into blood, before the great and the terrible day of the Lord come. And it shall come to pass, that whosoever shall call on the name of the Lord shall be delivered: for in mount Zion and in Jerusalem shall be deliverance, as the Lord hath said, and in the remnant whom the Lord shall call."*

Joel 2:27 - *"And ye shall know that I am in the midst of Israel, and that I am the Lord your God, and none else: and my people shall never be ashamed."* Could I say that just before the 400 years of silence which divides the Old Testament from the New Testament, God sent a race of mighty prophets to declare His truth to backsliding and apostate Israel.

The Old Testament finishes with their prophesies and many of them were contemporaries. Jeremiah was prophesying in Jerusalem while Joel was prophesying in Judah. Daniel was prophesying in Babylon at the same time as Jeremiah and Joel. Ezekiel was also prophesying in Babylon and also in the land.

The message of God's prophet is never popular. When the prophet becomes popular he ceases to be God's prophet. The prophet is the conveyor of God's judgment telegram. He is also the carrier and wielder of God's sword of judgment. However, the God whose sword he wields is still the God of mercy and judgment. As Isaiah tells us in 28:21, judgment is still His strange work.

Interspersed with all of these prophecies are wonderful promises of the all-merciful Jehovah God. Now you will notice in this chapter two of Joel you have this sounding of the trumpet. Look at chapter 21:1 *"Blow ye the trumpet in Zion"* and when you come down to verse 15 it says *"Blow the trumpet in Zion"*. Two trumpets, they remind us of Numbers 10:12 when under the Mosaic ritual two trumpets were used to the summoning of the people, and to their battle order when they went out to do warfare.

Coming after the sounding of this second trumpet in Joel we have a list of great encouraging promises of a mighty unstoppable revival work and the bursting forth from the lips of God's people appropriate praises to the God who sent it.

Notice the language of the verses which precede verse 27 and notice the language that comes after verse 27. It is actually the prophecy of the great

Christian Pentecost, the first Christian Pentecost which you can read about in Acts chapter two.

This text of mine is crammed full of the Being, the Attributes, the Uniqueness, the Singularity and the Sovereignty of Jehovah. You will notice, of course, that it commences with *"The Lord your God"*. LORD is in small capitals and in the Authorised Version that intimates that in the Hebrew text it is *Jehovah*.

Here we have God, the infinite God. Here we have God, the Father of spirits. Here we have God, the everlasting God. Here we have God, the unchangeable God. Here we have God, the only true God. Here we have God, the all-powerful God. Here we have God, the Thrice-Holy God. Here we have God, the Just God. Here we have God, the True God. Here we have God, the Only Wise God. For it is only that God who can reverse apostasy, backsliding and hellish darkness and say to a chaotic world "Let there be light" and light will come, the light of the glorious Gospel of Christ with revival power.

I remember as a little boy sitting at a radio to listen with bated breath to King George VI the father of our present Queen, as he broadcast on Christmas Day. Would to God she had the Christian faith that her father had. He said this, I never forgot it, "I said to the man which stood at the gate of the year, give me a light that I may tread safely into the unknown. And he said, go out and put your hand into the hand of God. That will be better to you than a light and safer than any known way."

It is about that God, who is better than a light and that God who is safer than any known way, of whom I want to speak.

If you look at the text you will find four things about God.

First of all you have **God's Presence**. *"Ye shall know that I am in the midst of Israel"*, God's Presence.

Second you have **God's Person**, *"I am the Lord your God"*.

Third you have **God's Power**, suggested in those words *"none else"* for no one else has the power to reverse the trends of apostasy. No one else can restore the years that have been eaten. Fourth, you have **God's Promise** *"my people shall never be ashamed"*.

Now if you look at those four things you will find the emphasis is on the centrality of God's Presence. What does it say? *"I am in the midst of Israel."* **The Centrality of God's Presence**. If you look at the second one you will find that there you have **The Responsibility of God's Person**. He is responsible for you and me. He is not just the Lord God but He is the Lord your God and I am glad God never forsakes His people. He is always with His people.

I was reading that great Psalm when the psalmist said, "Who will show us any good?" People say that to me every day. What is going to happen Dr Paisley? Who is going to help us? The Greatest of all Helpers - our God. He never forsakes His people.

Some Christians live as if God was dead but our God is a living God. The responsibility of God's Person.

Then you will notice that in the section of His Power, it is **The Reality of His Power**. There is none else like Him. There is no power like His Power.

The Secretary of this church said to me as we stood in the old church building. "I remember Sunday nights in this church when I could hear the breaking of the chains of sin around the hearts of sinners." I said, "Yes, that is true. Do you remember the night when the local RUC Sergeant from Willowfield and his wife came to the service to see what was happening, and do you remember how that big police officer was smitten with the power of God until he sobbed out in the meeting? Do you remember his wife? She was well prepared for the service. She had her painting and powdering well done but there were big streaks down her cheeks as she wept. When I made the appeal both of them staggered out and cried out to be saved. They were gloriously converted to Christ along with about a score of others on the same night." Yes, the reality of His Power.

Last of all, there is **The Unshakeability of His Promise** *"my people shall never be ashamed"*.

Now I would need a month to preach on this text. I want to draw your attention and I am skipping a lot of the preparation that I have done but I want to give you a thought. Start reading the New Testament and every time you find Jesus in the midst make a note of it. Now if you read it carefully you will find that six times in the Gospels Jesus was in the midst. Once in the book of the Revelation He was in the midst. He was in the midst of the Church. I am talking about Christ being in the midst of the Church. Of course, you will find that He was in the midst of the throne as well, in the book of Revelation. I am talking about God's presence among His people. Take your New Testament and turn to these Scriptures and mark them briefly. I am only going to make a very brief comment on them.

The first one is in Matthew 18:20, *"for where two or three are gathered together in my name there am I in the midst of them"* He is in the midst to **preside**. He takes the chair when God's people meet. He is there to preside. In the midst to preside. The presiding presence.

Turn to Luke 2:46, the first reference to Christ after the purification of His mother in the temple and you will find another verse concerning the Lord Jesus Christ, *"and it came to pass that after three days they found him in the temple sitting in the midst of the doctors both hearing them and asking them questions."* He hears us and He questions us. In the midst to **probe**.

Then turn to Luke 5:19 and you will find that Jesus was in the house, and they brought the man with the palsy and they could not get him to Jesus so they took the tiles off the flat roof and they made a big gaping hole. It was well that they did not have rain like we have or they would have been flooded out! They let down the man sick of the palsy. Where did they leave him, put him down? It says *"in the midst before Jesus"*. What did Jesus say to him? Jesus said to him a simple word *"Man, thy sins are forgiven thee"*. He is in the midst to **pardon**. Where the Lord is there is His pardoning presence. It is a great thing to know His presiding presence. It is a great thing to know His probing presence. It is a great thing to know His pardoning presence.

Turn over to John's Gospel 8:3, *"and they took this woman, taken with adultery and they set her in the midst where Jesus was and they say unto him, Master this woman was taken in adultery, in the very act."* If she had been taken in adultery in the very act why was not the adulterer, the man, not taken? You see this was a put up job and we discover that the Lord Jesus said, *"he that is without sin among you let him first cast a stone at her"*. They heard it and being convicted by their own conscience, went out one by one, beginning at the eldest even unto the last. The Lord Jesus Christ is in the midst to **penalise**. He does the right judgment. You will not have any cover-up with the Lord. You will not get away from sinning when the Lord comes in the midst. He will root out the sin. He will root out every form of bitterness that will rise up. He will make the judgment. You need to accept the judgment of the Lord.

Some people make their own judgments and then they think that God should say amen to their judgments. No such thing. God only says amen to His own judgments. When the Lord looked at this woman, what did He say? He said, *"Neither do I condemn you."* He is in the midst to penalise.

Turn to John 19:18 where *"where they crucified him and two other with him, on either side one and Jesus in the midst"*. What was He there to do? He was there to propitiate, to **pay** the price of our sins.

Lifted up was He to die.
"It is finished" was His cry.
Now in heaven exalted high,
Hallelujah what a Saviour!

You know we have a false gospel being preached today that men's faith becomes their righteousness. You will not find one word about that in the Bible. Our righteousness is the righteousness of Jesus Christ. He is made unto us wisdom, righteousness, sanctification and redemption. Not only so, He was made sin for us that knew no sin, that we might be made the righteousness of God in Him. When you put on Christ, hallelujah! you put on righteousness. You get the glorious white coat that you need. If you read the book of Revelation you will find that every time the clothing of the saints is mentioned, they are clothed in white linen, which is the righteousness of saints. That is the righteousness of Christ. I go into heaven robed in the righteousness that God takes out of His wardrobe, the righteousness of His Son. I got that new suit, thank God, one day at the Cross and there is not a stain or a mark upon it. It is unstainable, it cannot be marked. It is the precious righteousness of Christ. That is why I don't need a bachelor priest. That is why I don't need a confessional box. That is why I don't need a mass. That is why I don't need an idol. That is why I need no priest or pastor or prelate or preacher. I have Christ, what want I more? Nothing but the blood of Jesus and the righteousness of the Son of God. In the midst to **propitiate**.

Then He is in the midst to proclaim. Luke 24:36 with two parallel passages John 30:19-20. What does it say there in Luke's Gospel? It tells me in verse 36 *"as they thus spake, Jesus himself stood in the midst of them, and saith unto them, Peace be unto you. But they were terrified and affrighted, and supposed that they had seen a spirit. And He said unto them, Why are ye troubled, and why do thoughts arise in your hearts?"* What did He come to do? He came to proclaim His resurrection and He said, *"Behold my hands and my feet, that it is I myself."* Jesus Christ comes among His people to **proclaim** that He is the great resurrection and the life.

If you turn over to the first chapter of the book of Revelation you will remember that He appeared unto John He said, *"I am Alpha and Omega, the first and the last."* When John turned he saw Him and when he saw Him he fell at His feet as dead. What did He say, He said, *"Fear not, I am He that liveth and was dead; and behold I am alive for evermore."* Hallelujah! Jesus is alive.

We do not worship a dead Christ. Rome presents Christ in every act of her worship as an impotent, powerless Christ. He has to be held up in His mother's arms. He is impotent. He has to be held up upon a cross. He is impotent. He has to be held up in the tomb. Those are the three things that Rome presents but we today know that He came and was born of a pure virgin. She was a sinner and she got saved through Christ for she said, *"My spirit hath rejoiced in God my Saviour."* If she was immaculately born she would not have needed to be saved but, praise God, she was saved like anybody else, trusting in Christ alone. He is no longer on the cross. Thank God He is not nailed to a cross today. Away with the crucifix. It is a blasphemy and insult to the risen Saviour. He is alive for ever more. Praise God He is not in the tomb. I was at that tomb and He was not there. It said on the door of it *"He is not here, He is risen."* Praise God, I shouted hallelujah! There was a Church of England minister with me and he nearly fell. He nearly took fright. He nearly died when he heard a Free Presbyterian shouting a good hallelujah! Jesus is alive! He is a living Christ. That is what we are preaching. Oh it is a great thing, is it not, to have Christ in the midst of us to preside, to pardon, to penalise, to propitiate, to proclaim.

Then in the book of the Revelation He is in the midst among the churches walking in judgment. What is He doing? He is purifying the churches. When Jesus comes He comes to purify.

That is the first point of this sermon, just about half delivered. Let me just mention one thing to you. This name Jehovah. The responsibility of His person. The word Jehovah occurs in the Old Testament and it occurs in a compound way. There are many Jehovahs compounded with another word.

I was studying and having a fresh look at Psalm 23 and I discovered that Psalm 23 is an exposition of seven compound words Jehovah. How does it start off? *"The Lord is my Shepherd I shall not want"* He is Jehovah Jireh. Genesis 22:14 *"the Lord will provide"*. *"He maketh me to lie down in green pastures, he leadeth me beside the still waters"* Jehovah Shalom, Judges 6:24 *"the Lord will give peace"*.

Then we come to the next verse in the Psalm. What is the next verse of Psalm 23? You will note carefully the order in which they come. *"He restoreth my soul, he leadeth me in the paths of righteousness"*. Here we have two compound names of Jehovah in action. Exodus 15:26 Jehovah Ropheka *"he restoreth my soul"* Jehovah Tsidkenu. That is in Jeremiah 23:6 *"the Lord our righteousness"* *"he leadeth me in the paths of righteousness"*. So He is Jehovah Jireh, the Lord will provide. He is Jehovah Shalom, the Lord will give peace. He is Jehovah Ropheka, the Lord that healeth thee. He is Jehovah Tsidkenu, the Lord our righteousness.

But come with me to verse four, what does it say there? *"Yea, though I walk through the valley of the shadow of death, I will fear no evil for thou art with me"*. He is Jehovah Shammah. Ezekiel 48:15 Jehovah is there.

Then He is Jehovah my banner and you will read about that in Exodus 17:35, Jehovah Nissi, the Lord our banner. What does it say in Psalm 23 verse 5? *"thou preparest a table before me in the presence of my enemies"*. He brought me into His banqueting house and His banner over me was love. The first chapter of the Canticles, the Song of Solomon. Seventhly, in Exodus 31:13 He is Jehovah Mekaddishkem, which means the Lord that separates thee. How does the Lord separate us? He anoints our head with oil and He gives us the overflowing cup. The sinner has not the Lord's anointing and the sinner does not have the cup of blessing but thank God I have that.

So we have the seven-fold fulfilment in that Psalm and that means the Lord is responsible for me. I don't need the health services to look after me, the Lord will provide for me. I don't need the cares of men. You know, David said. *"Once I was young and now I am old* (and many of us can say that today), *but I have not seen the righteous forsaken nor his seed begging bread."* The Lord will provide. He is all these things. "I am the Lord your God."

You know, Paul enters into an argument in Romans chapter eight and he says, "Who is he that condemneth? It is Christ that died. Who is he that brings accusations? It is God that justifies." I depend not on myself, I depend wholly on the Lord. I am His child. Therefore, I should be under His care and I should not try to care for myself, for the Lord will take care of me. None else has power.

I would like you to go home and look at the previous verses. You will find the giving of rain, the glories of harvest, the grace of restoration and the greatness of the provision, it is all there in those verses.

Last of all, we have the unshakeability of His **promise**. *"God speaketh once, yea twice, but man perceiveth it not that power belongeth unto God."* Do you notice the verse 26 of Joel chapter 2 repeats the promise which we have in verse 27, *"My people shall never be ashamed"*. God's people will never be ashamed. I would like to shout it in the ear of the World Council of Churches. I would like to shout it in the ear of those people who said this church could never erect a church complex but God's people will never be ashamed. If you are in the centre of God's will, with Christ in the vessel you can smile at the storm as you go sailing home.

May God indeed bless us and keep us and cause His face to shine upon us. Are you glad you are saved today? Are you glad you are happy in Christ and you have not a big long face, as Dr Bob used to tell us, you could drink buttermilk out of the churn without tipping it up. No, we are not like that! We are rejoicing! The best is yet to be! We are only starting. I wish I was only 20 again and starting on this road again but that cannot be done. But God says, I will restore the years that the locusts have eaten. He is a miracle-working God.

Lord, do miracles amongst us for Jesus Sake!

AMEN AND AMEN!

Index
to texts

APPENDIX ONE

Glorying in the Cross

A SERMON PREACHED BY DR. PAISLEY ON 17 FEBRUARY, 1963
IN RAVENHILL FREE PRESBYTERIAN CHURCH

"But God forbid that I should glory, save in the cross of our Lord Jesus Christ, by whom the world is crucified unto me, and I unto the world." (Galatians 6:14).

OURS IS A LAODICEAN AGE. Apostate Protestantism like Apostate Romanism is given to glorying in the things of this present evil world. The world patronised churches of today glory in tradition. "Look at our history", they exclaim. "See the mighties listed in our annals. Surely we are the true church."

They glory in *buildings*. They point to their magnificent ecclesiastical structures. They are proud of their architectural glory, a glory that is Gothic, Grecian, Georgian or Contemporary, (shall I say contemptuous?)

They glory in *numbers*. They can blind you with statistics and stagger you with their long lists of subscribers. How many of these actually attend the Sunday services we wot not but we wonder!

They glory in *finances*. They are rich and increased with goods and have need of nothing. Their church budgets swell year by year. Their investments are colossal.

They glory in *learning*. Their schools and colleges are unparalleled. Theirs are the great men with the highest educational attainments.

They glory in their *standing*. Theirs are the recognised churches. "Why," they proudly declare, "the very mention of our name is honourable. We are no mere sect, no sir, we are the church."

My language is entirely different. With the rugged and scarred apostle I can say, "But God forbid that I should glory, save in the cross of our Lord Jesus Christ, by whom the world is crucified unto me, and I unto the world," Yes,

All of what the world doth boast
I have learned to count but loss,
And the sight that charms me most
Is a sinner at the Cross.

I I WILL GLORY IN THE DESCRIPTION OF THE CROSS
"the cross our Lord Jesus Christ"

Paul's description is worthy of attention. It is not merely the cross of Jesus or the cross of the Lord or the cross of Christ. It is more, it is the cross of the *Lord Jesus Christ*. Yes, but even then the description is not complete. It is the cross of *our* Lord Jesus Christ. There is an important and distinguishing relationship here which must not be overlooked.

Firstly, His Deity is Emphasised.

He is called "Lord". The Lord of the New Testament is the Jehovah of the Old. The emphasis is upon the Saviour's Deity. Herein lies the might of the cross. The Cross is a demonstration of might. That sacrifice on yonder tree is unique. It is both unnatural and supernatural. In all the annals of history and in all the unfolding of things yet to be, never again will there be such a sacrifice.

Well may the sun in darkness hide
And shut his glories in,
When God the mighty maker died
For man the creature's sin.

Sinner, behold and repent. God Incarnate suffered on the Cross. Saint, behold and rejoice. God Incarnate has atoned completely for thy sins.

Secondly, His Humanity is Emphasised

He is called "Jesus". The emphasis is upon Our Lord's humanity. Herein lies the mystery of the cross. The cross is a declaration of mystery, the mystery of godliness, God manifest in the flesh. The purpose of the incarnation is propitiation. To this end was He born. He became flesh in order to die. He entered into time in order to redeem. He came into the world of sinners in order to save. He was crucified in order to justify.

Thirdly, His Office is Emphasised

He is called "Christ". Christ means the Anointed One, the emphasis is on His office. Herein lies the mercy of the cross. The cross is a proclamation of mercy.

In the Old Testament, prophets, priests and kings entered upon their special offices by anointing. Christ, who is our Prophet, Priest and King entered upon these three great offices as mediator by a special anointing. He is truly Christ the Anointed One, anointed with the oil of gladness above His fellows for the Holy Spirit was not given by measure unto Him.

Away in eternity, in the everlasting Council Chamber of the Holy Three, Jehovah the Father laid hold upon Jehovah the Son and by Jehovah the Holy Ghost anointed and appointed Him as the only Redeemer of the elect.

Behold Him in eternity, the anointed Prophet, Priest and King of His people. Yes, but come to Calvary, where hangs the anointed Prophet; hear His prayers from the cross. There hangs the anointed Priest; behold His priestly work in awful sacrifice upon the tree. There hangs the anointed King crowned with thorns; wonder at His Kingly power in glorious display from that strange throne of wood. He raiseth the vilest offender, the dying thief, to peerage of heaven. This is mercy indeed. The cross is the cross of Christ, the Lord Jesus Christ.

Fourth, His Relationship is Emphasised

He is *our* Lord Jesus Christ. He, our Lord Jesus Christ, has brought those who are saved into an intimate, personal and glorious relationship with Himself. Herein lies the *majesty* of the cross. The cross is a revelation of majesty.

The redeemed of the Lord revel in such language as that of the saintly Rutherford.

Oh, I am my beloved's
And my beloved's mine;
He brings a poor vile sinner
Into His house of wine.

I stand upon His merit,
I know no safer stand
Not even where glory dwelleth,
In Emmanuel's land.

The cross is the cross of *our* Lord, our Lord Jesus Christ.

II I WILL GLORY IN THE DEATH OF THE CROSS
"the cross"

Paul had no hazy ideas of what he meant by the cross. Even a casual study of his writings will make that perfectly plain. The great apostle gloried not in the sign of the cross but rather in the sacrifice of the cross, not in the emblem of the cross but rather in the expiation of the cross, not in the structure of the cross but rather in the salvation of the cross, and not in the wood of the cross but rather in the work of the cross.

The argument often used in Protestant circles that the emblem of an empty cross is the proper sign of Christ's finished work is completely foreign to the Scriptures of Truth. Its origin is pagan and popish.

The Lord Jesus Christ Himself has given to us divinely appointed emblems of His death and finished work - the bread and wine of the communion feast. Any other emblems are an insult to His last commands, and are the furniture of Bethaven, the house of idols. The use of the emblem of the cross and the sign of the cross in many professed Protestant Churches is a sad departure from the glorious principles of our great Reformed heritage, a retrograde step in the direction of the Woman of Babylon.

The cross to the Apostle meant simply "a living Saviour dying that a dying sinner might live." All Paul's writings are an exposition and elucidation of this tremendous theme. This is the pith and marrow, the cream and essence of his whole theology. What wonderful definitions he gives us of the great doctrines of the cross.

Of **Imputation** he says, *"For He hath made him to be sin for us, who knew no sin; that we might be made the righteousness of God in him."* 2 Cor. 5:21.
Of **Substitution** he writes: *"the Son of God, who loved me, and gave himself for me."* Gal. 2:20
Of **Reconciliation** he declares: *" God was in Christ, reconciling the world unto himself."* 2. Cor. 5:19.

Of **Redemption** he proclaims, "*In whom we have redemption through his blood, the forgiveness of sins, according to the riches of his grace.*"
Eph. 1:7
Of **Salvation** he speaks, "*This is a faithful saying, and worthy of all acceptation, that Christ Jesus came into the world to save sinners; of whom I am chief.*"
I Tim. 1:15

Here then was what Paul glorified in and I too would make this the theme of all my glorying. What else dare poor bankrupt sinners glory in? We need grace, the cross is the great fount of grace. We need forgiveness, the cross is the great bank of forgiveness. We need hope, the cross is the great anchor of hope. We need power, the cross is the great generator of power. We need a way to heaven. The cross is the great ladder to glory.

> *Stretched on the cross, the Saviour dies,*
> *Hark! His expiring groans arise!*
> *See from His hands, His feet, His side,*
> *Runs down the sacred crimson tide!*
> *But life attends the deathful sound,*
> *And flows from every bleeding wound;*
> *The vital stream, how free it flows,*
> *To save and cleanse His rebel foes!*

III I WILL GLORY IN THE DIMENSIONS OF THE CROSS
"the Cross"

The cross is a mighty thing and it has tremendous dimensions.

The Height of the Cross - The Cross Godward

At the top of the accursed tree are the nail-pierced hands of the Godman. Heaven's doors are barred to me, the law condemned sinner. Divine justice has fastened up the eternal chains and turned the everlasting lock against my entrance. The top of the cross is the golden key and those bleeding hands are the power that turns it in the lock.

Behold, the golden key is fitted in the lock. Behold those blessed hands turning it. See the great chains lifted down. Hear the glad sound of the unlocking of heaven's gate. Wonder, the blessed portals are thrown back. Rejoice, by grace from the top of the cross I step onto Jehovah's throne, the heir of God and joint heir of Christ.

The Centre of the cross - The Cross Christward

At the centre of the cross is the broken heart of Christ, flowing crimson for the sins of His people. He is now fulfilling His covenant engagements for and on behalf of His own. He is now drinking the bitter cup of judgment that we might partake of the blessed cup of justification. He bleeds in order to bless. He suffers that we might be saved. He dies that we might live.

Jesus, Thou Son and heir of heaven,
Thou spotless Lamb of God!
I see Thee bathed in sweat and tears,
And sweltering in Thy blood!
He died, that we to sin might die,
And live to God alone;
He died, our hearts to purify
And make them all His own.

The Breadth of the Cross - The Cross Manward

The limits of the cross are the sides of the Blessed Redeemer. From His wounded side there flows a veritable torrent of blood, forming a sea of mercy without bottom, brim or shore. East and west, north and south it flows bringing redemption to the world of sinners. 'Neath those crimson waves there is cleansing for you, dear sinner. Yes, you can sail to the promised land of the heavenly Canaan on the Red Sea of the Redeemer's blood. Plunge at once beneath this fountain and then in glad experience you will shout, Hallelujah to the Lamb!

The Base of the Cross - The Cross Devilward

At the base of the cross are the bleeding feet to Jesus. Yes, the adder was bruising his heel, but, praise God, the adder's head was crushed beneath His feet. The gospel promise given at the dawning of man's sinful history is gloriously fulfilled. The great adversary of God and man is vanquished by the victorious Christ. The Lion of Judah is conqueror o'er the dragon of the pit. The Stone of Zion smashed the serpent of hell. With old Newton we can sing:

> *Satan and his host, amazed,*
> *Saw this Stone in Zion laid;*
> *Jesus, though to death abased,*
> *Bruised the subtle serpent's head,*
> *When, to save us,*
> *On the cross His blood He shed.*

IV. I WILL GLORY IN THE DESIGN OF THE CROSS
"by whom the world is crucified unto me and I unto the world."

Why, we have the design of the cross revealed in the mysterious fact that upon it were three crucifixions all in one!

Christ was crucified, that's substitution

He took my place and died for me. Upon that basis I, a totally condemned, heart condemned, heaven condemned sinner, am justified freely by His grace. No more wrath for me. No more hell for me. No more condemnation for me. Only mercy, heaven and pardon for my soul. Hosanna to the Son of David!

I am crucified, that's identification

Christ not only died for me but He died as me. He was my representative as well as my substitute. In Him I died and so in Him I live for evermore. He that is dead is freed from sin. Behold the shining way to victory, the King's Highway of life everlasting. Sinner, this is the way from the dungeon to the palace, from imprisonment to enthronement.

The world is crucified, that's emancipation

The power of the world is broken. Its siren song is stilled in silence. Its allurements have become the corruption of the tomb. Its entertainments the rattling bones and the grinning of the skulls. Its bloom is paled in death, its beauties despoiled by the decay of the grave. The world that I once thought so lovely, so enchanting, so intriguing is now by the cross a vile stinking corpse. I hurl it from me, ashamed I ever found it lovely. I repudiate its claims, surprised that I should ever have been enticed by its temptations. I am emancipated from the world, it is crucified unto me.

Alas, some of you are still held by the power of the world. Poor fools, running after a bubble which will soon burst and vanish from your enchanted eyes. Through the cross there is deliverance for you. Right now by that wondrous cross you can become a new creature and all your old sinful desires, habits, practices and language can be gone forever. Turn now and flee to the cross, look not behind you lest you be consumed.

THE
❧ IAN R. K. PAISLEY LIBRARY ❧

OTHER BOOKS IN THIS SPECIAL SERIES

♦ **Christian Foundations**

♦ **An Exposition of the Epistle to the Romans**

♦ **The Garments of Christ**

♦ **Sermons on Special Occasions**

♦ **Expository Sermons**

♦ **A Text a Day keeps the Devil Away**

♦ **The Rent Veils at Calvary**

♦ **My Plea for the Old Sword**

❧ AVAILABLE FROM ❧

AMBASSADOR PRODUCTIONS, ltd.

**Providence House
16 Hillview Avenue,
Belfast, BT5 6JR
Telephone: 01232 658462**

**Emerald House
1 Chick Springs Road, Suite 102
Greenville, South Carolina, 29609
Telephone: 1 800 209 8570**